Wondrous Wildlife

A Different Look

Published by
MONTANA
MAGAZINE

by **GEORGE OSTROM**

and **Ranger Shannon Ostrom**

Page 1: **SWIFTCURRENT BULL** *Summer's the time for all ungulates (split-hoofed animals) to regrow their antlers, and this bull moose developed a dandy pair in 1997. We saw him when he was a two-year-old and noted the above-average body size. Here he is grown up, with horns still in August velvet, king of the Swiftcurrent Valley. In spring of that year, a cow moose with two calves was feeding in Swiftcurrent Lake when a grizzly bear charged out of the forest, killed and carried away one of the calves—while frightened Glacier Park tourists were watching.*

Such things are a natural part of the prey/predator relationship, but humans are seldom around to witness. Full-grown bull moose like this one have few enemies to fear, but wolf packs and mountain lions can bring them down, especially when they are old or in poor physical condition. An old-time trapper told us of finding a large bull killed by a desperately hungry young female mountain lion that managed to leap on the bull's back from a rock ledge and bite through the vertebrae behind the head.

Front cover (top right): **GLOWING YELLOW VEST AND BLACK V'D BREAST** *No other lark sings as often or as long as the one they call "meadow." Expanding towns and cities are decreasing their habitat, but thankfully there are still thousands of square miles of open land for them...at least in the West.*

Front cover (center): **"THE BEAR THAT WALKS LIKE A MAN."** *Grizzlies stand on hing legs to see farther, but they charge on all fours. This young adult male had never seen "the oldest living reporter" before, and wanted a second look. George thinks it's his best wild griz shot. Been closer a few times, but camera flaws caused mysterious shaking. A rare photo-op near Many Glacier road, June 18, 1998.*

Front cover (lower left): **THAT'S NO HORSE** *Notice how this old ram is deliberately keeping his head turned away from the sign. We're pretty sure he can't read, but it does look a little suspicious. The Park Service could solve this problem by erecting a few "Sheep Crossing" signs in the area.*

Back cover: **ON THE LAM** *After around eighteen months with their mothers, mountain lions are put out to find their own territory. That is when they usually get into trouble, because food may be hard to find. This young male adult was caught in a rural hen house, and dogs chased it up a tree. After everyone left, he came down and ran away. Lions are naturally very shy and avoid human contact.*

In northwest Montana where we live, lions have increased in number as whitetail deer populations have risen, and that causes a new problem, because more humans are also choosing to live in rural forests. In the last fifteen years, lion attacks on humans have occurred, including one case where a small boy was killed near a house and carried away into the forest. Glacier Park has recorded two attacks on children, and elsewhere incidents have soared. Between midsummer 1997 and June of '98, more than a dozen lions were shot for eating pets and threatening people in neighboring Flathead County. The problem is also developing in other western states.

Bounties were paid on lions in Montana until 1962, and they were still fair game for anyone to shoot until 1971, when they were declared an official protected big game animal. Now populations are managed by state government, which runs controlled hunting by permits and quotas. Shannon and I together have seen less than ten in our total of over a hundred years in the wilds. George's son-in-law, Shawn Price, killed one with a bow and arrow, and it qualified for the Boone and Crockett world records. It was getting old and likely would have moved into settled areas to find easier prey such as domestic colts, house cats or pet dogs.

In good health, the cougar, puma or mountain lion is an amazing beast completely designed for successful hunting, and can bring down animals five times its own weight. Like all cats, they are very curious, and as a young man living in the mountains, George often saw where a lion had picked up his tracks in the snow and followed for a considerable distance. Knowing there were no verified cases of these big cats attacking people at that time, he was not concerned.

Right: **PEEKABOO** *Some call great horned owls the winged tiger, wingspan to fifty-five inches. As a boy, Shannon roamed the river bottom near our home and found many wild things to study. In years of short food supply, strongest nestlings may shove weaker ones out to perish—population control at a basic level. This one has a few more weeks to get rid of the fuzzy kid feathers and start flying lessons.*

CONTENTS

DEDICATION

She has stood in the door a thousand times. From her heart she said, "You be careful, George." One day it changed: "George, you take good care of that little boy." In following years we heard: "George, take good care of those little boys." For the last twenty-five years she said, "You guys be careful."

This book is dedicated to Iris.

Above: **THE GOOD LIFE** *Monster meadows of green grass and flowers, babbling brooks and shady forests give this whitetail buck the good life. Fawns and does aren't the only members of this species that like to play. One of Shannon's friends was sitting by a road one cold fall morning when he heard a tinkling sound like breaking glass. He peeked around the corner and saw a big buck like this one wandering all over the road, breaking the ice on each frozen puddle.*

Facing page: **FALL PTARMIGAN** *Autumn in alpine country means the wild ptarmigan is turning snow white as Mother Nature prepares her winter camouflage. It snowed up there the next day and we wondered if the poor bird had to lie on his back until the top half got white.*

The purpose of this book is to entertain with photos and interesting stories of the wild creatures my son Shannon and I have been watching all our lives in the western U.S. and Canada. It is a fascinating activity, and wondrous times last longer when they are shared.

Besides being beautiful, funny, serious and amazing, our friends in wild places do have complex individual personalities, moods and traits. These characteristics provide constant surprises.

Animals make plans, solve problems, enjoy playing games and respond to outside stimuli with anger, flight, curiosity or disdain. They have laws regulating territory and social behavior and, like humans, they sometimes get into trouble by breaking rules of the wild or of their own common sense. They can be affectionate or passive, aggressive and dangerous. Some are tamable…most are not. They may flee in discretion or fight to the death. All wild things display imagination and inventiveness and, like humans, take joy when it comes, and adjust to bad times.

Few wild creatures, predators or prey, die of old age, but they do not sit around contemplating death in the manner of *homo sapiens*. Ernest Seton-Thompson went so far as to say, "The life of a wild animal always has a tragic end." That view seems severe in human terms. To animals, life is for living and just as it is with every living thing, death is fundamental, the inevitable end of life.

One hundred years ago, Seton-Thompson began publishing books about animals using his artistic talent to richly illustrate each volume. The first, in 1898, was *Wild Animals I Have Known*. His huge public success helped change the way millions of people now look at our untamed friends.

Seton-Thompson pushed theory to the limit by attributing to animals such complex human characteristics as heartbreak, hate, and suicide. His personal approach was labeled outrageous anthropomorphism by critics. However, that noted naturalist did capture the hearts of several generations, thus helping to encourage serious research into whether animals are "simplistic organic machines, inflexibly programmed by evolution" or more akin to humans than once believed.

On the wondrous side, the mammals and birds in this book come equipped with mysterious talents, instincts and biological mechanisms so complex they defy explanation or understanding by the most brilliant of today's scientists. The authors of this book make no pretense at high falutin' theories or uncommon knowledge. We watch, take pictures, and wonder.

We hope our book gives readers a better understanding of wild creatures' lives, but more importantly, instills a deeper appreciation of man's priceless gift— sharing the world with other amazing living things.

—*George Ostrom*

5

AUTUMN IS GOOD *When daylight hours grow shorter and the nights get colder, all living things react. Leaves start turning, birds make travel plans and the big creatures prepare for two things: the season of romance...and coming winter. Those goats up by the cliff will stay right here enjoying the scenery, pairing up and staying out of bad winds.*

INTRODUCTION

Grizzly bears and bighorn rams can't read highway signs. Ravens don't tinker with motorcycles. Shannon and I didn't do this book to promote such crazy ideas, but there's little harm in having fun with pictures and stories that seem to say they can. Our hope is readers of all ages will feel the fun and share our awe of all wild things, from the littlest owl to the biggest bull moose.

You do not get photos of bison covered with ice unless you put on skis and go out in -42° F. weather, and the only way to see how the bighorn sheep are doing in February is to climb half frozen and look; on the flip side, what beats lying in a sunny meadow watching blue-birds or hiking a high autumn ridge where bull elk bugle until the mountains ring?

Shannon and I are hunters, fishermen, mountain climbers, skiers and world travelers; but above all else, we watch wild things. Wasn't planned, just happened. Aiding and abetting this activity is our living in Kalispell, Montana, between the National Bison Range and Glacier National Park. A one-day drive puts us in Jasper, Alberta, or south to Yellowstone and Grand Teton national parks, and we are surrounded by six giant National Wilderness Areas.

Naturally, we've had scary moments, sad times when seeing birds and beasts in tragic situations, but mostly these years with binoculars and cameras have been a great joy.

The results of all this are thousands of photos that don't do much good for anyone unless they are in a book. Also, Shannon's mother Iris, my wife, has long suggested we start doing something with our wildlife hobby that makes a few bucks along with costing so much.

This book is for you…and for Iris.

BOTTOM OF THE FOOD CHAIN *Columbian ground squirrels reproduce by the thousands because that is their job. Pioneers shot hawks, owls, coyotes and so many other predators that gophers and similar rodents multiplied by the millions. Their numbers threatened farm crops. In the 1940s there were good summer jobs for high schoolers spreading poisoned oats for these small critters. America is moving more toward natural balance, so with the big raptors increasing in numbers there is less need for rodent eradication programs. In the national parks, where the food chain is fairly well intact, these squirrels are the main food of many hunting birds as well as the smaller four-footed predators. Also on a bottom rung is the prolific rabbit family. Luckily, Mother Nature uses an active hare restorer.*

ON HER OWN *Last spring's kid hasn't started to shed its first winter coat, but will soon. She stayed with her mother through the winter, but with a kid brother or sister coming any day, she's on her own; however, goats are social animals and in high summer pastures we've seen up to fifty of them together, old and young, males and females. Have also observed yearlings join the mother's new family and even do some baby-sitting.*

Above: **POLISHING THE DAGGERS**
Trees and brush take a heck of a beating when bull elk shed velvet off antlers and start polishing up the tines. They aren't just beating the bushes for fun. They're also practicing for battle, strengthening neck muscles and getting the old adrenaline going. At times they'll get as worked up over slashing a small tree as they would fighting for a world championship.

Right: **BULL WITH VELVET ANTLERS**
Summer's the time bull elk grow new antlers to replace those shed in late winter. This bull is also still shedding the last of his winter coat. We remember this one because he was killed that fall fighting with another bull over who got to romance the neighborhood females. It happened on the National Bison Range.

A Spine-Tingling Elk

It took a few years before George saw any humor in the experience, but one of his most spine-tingling adventures with wild animals involved a large bull elk.

One summer long ago, when there were no TVs, PCs, CDs, or 16-ounce Coke bottles, I lied just a bit about my age and went to work for the U.S. Forest Service as a "smoke chaser." After finishing Fire School at a ranger station, I was sent back into the boonies of the Flathead National Forest for road and trail work. I stayed at a log bunkhouse in a primitive land with abundant wildlife. Along the narrow dead-end road to Spotted Bear, two cars a day was considered unusual traffic.

One August evening our crew was sitting on the porch watching thunderheads roll in from the west over Tom Tom and Three Eagles mountains. A few lightning flashes began to crack along high ridges as the storm moved toward us. Then, from out of nowhere, a big bolt bored into the forest across and up river. Within minutes smoke began curling up.

We telephoned the ranger station, and a dispatcher told Foreman Buck to take one man and go over there. We young fellas considered Buck to be an elderly person because he was the same age as our dads, too old for The War. He looked over our green group and asked, "Which one of you men is going to help me put out that fire?" I couldn't volunteer fast enough. "Okay, Ostrom," he said. "Get two packs from the fire cache and get in the gravel truck."

We drove to the only bridge and headed up the river's west side toward the strike. I was anxious to see my first forest fire action, but when we came around a corner near Wheeler Creek, there were two big bull elk fighting in the middle of the road. Buck slammed on the brakes and said, "Never saw 'em goin' at it this early before." The bulls completely ignored us until one seemed to win the battle and turned from his retreating foe. He trotted toward us and lowered his head, swinging that ominous rack of horns back and forth while snorting and pawing the ground.

Buck put the truck in low and started moving it slowly toward the enraged bull.

"What are you going to do, Buck?"

"I'm goin' to push him out of the way. We have to get to that fire." Buck shoved against the elk's horns a bit, and that made the bull madder. Several times he hooked tines under the bumper and rocked that twelve-ton truck up and down like a teeter-totter.

Buck appeared to be having the greatest moment of his Forest Service career, but I was uneasy. "Does this sort of thing happen a lot up here, Buck?"

"Nope. First time I ever heard of a bull elk taking on a truck. Kinda fun, huh?"

"If you win, are you going to marry a couple of the cows?"

"Don't get funny, Ostrom, or I'll throw you out of the cab."

After several shoves that skidded the bull backwards, Buck put the truck in reverse to let the elk think it might be winning. This push and shove went on for about ten minutes. Just when the bull seemed ready for a truce, Buck honked. That started the fight all over again. Bull elk must not like the sound of a 1939 truck horn. Buck finally shoved the bull backwards hard enough to end the fray with the elk scrambling clear of the bumper. He stood bugling and pawing the ground beside the road as we drove away.

Maybe a mile farther on we came to the fire, burning in roots and duff at the bottom of a dead spruce snag, a hundred yards off the road. In less than an hour we had dug a line down to mineral soil around the area and started separating the burning fuels from the unburned stuff. In another hour it was getting dark, and Buck said, "Well, kid, this fire isn't going anyplace. But one of us should stay here through the night, just to make sure."

Even without a high school diploma, I knew who was going to stay and who was going to sleep in a bed that night.

About midnight I curled up under the canvas used to wrap fire tools, but I soon was chilled. I got up and tried to find some fire we hadn't put out, but was unsuccessful. I did locate warm ashes and dirt, so I made a mattress out of that mixture and dozed off. I woke up scared…a rutting bull elk had grunted from trees near

the road. "Holy cow!" I thought. "Buck gets that big devil all riled up, then leaves me here alone."

I turned on my flashlight and climbed a fir tree. Though I didn't have a watch, I figured it was around 2 a.m. Perching buns on a limb in the middle of the night gets less and less fun by the minute. I hung on for quite a while before coming down just in time to hear loud snaps from breaking branches and something moving through the brush. I swiftly climbed back up the tree, staying up there an hour the second time. All the while I was trying unsuccessfully to do what one of the old-timers advised: "Shiver yourself warm."

I remembered there were matches in the fire pack. After the woods had been quiet for a spell, I came down and started a bonfire inside the fire line. The flames were soon warm and cheerful, but Kid Ostrom wasn't a happy camper, jumping at sounds from the darkness while the minutes and hours dragged by.

Buck showed up shortly after daylight, bringing hard-boiled eggs, semi-warm bacon, cold toast with jelly, and coffee. While I was gulping that down, he asked how things had gone out there in the bush, and I mumbled, "Fine. Just fine."

"Well, I'm glad to hear that, George. After I got back to the bunkhouse, I had a little trouble gettin' to sleep. Got to thinkin' that crazy bull might accidentally wander over

THERE'S A GOOSE IN THE GRASS *Just like all young animals, a calf elk has great curiosity about its fellow creatures. That's how they learn. This one has lost its spring spots but it is still exploring the world. Shannon thought maybe it was part English pointer because of this near perfect point. We couldn't help but discuss whether or not the calf could be taught to retrieve. Probably not.*

here and run you up a tree. Almost got up and drove back but then remembered I've never heard of an elk attacking a human, so I was able to get some rest."

"Thanks, Buck, but aren't you the same guy who told me last night that you'd never heard of one attacking a truck?"

Above: **FATHER OF MANY** *The fall elk family consists of a bull and his harem of cows, some with last spring's calves. Female elk do not mate until the second fall. While we were watching this group, another large bull came bugling and running over the nearby ridge. This one strolled out to meet the challenge and the other bull decided to go back where he came from. The ongoing bugling of bull elk can make the mountains ring, and almost shake the ground, especially if several are bugling at the same time. The sounds start low and rise to a high-pitched crescendo, often followed by grunts that can border on roars. It is a language of warning, challenge, and a call for love. Once heard…never forgotten.*

Right: **I'M READY** *Here is a bull with only five points per beam, but his rack is big and heavy. He is a magnificent animal, fitter than many mature bulls with six or more points. The dagger tines are two feet long—wicked weapons. During the rutting season he collected a good harem of cows and fought off several rivals that had more points.*

Above: **CONFUSED YOUNG ELK** *The first time we saw this yearling bull feeding with free-roaming range cattle we figured he was just passing through, but he stuck around as summer went along. It is not rare for wild animals to make friends with domestic critters, but this one seemed to think he was one of 'em. There are wild herds of elk in this area but maybe this one just liked tamer company. Saw the rancher in town and warned him to not be surprised if one or two of his heifers had a funny looking calf the next spring.*

Left: **USING HIS HORNS** *Because of too many elk for the winter ranges in Yellowstone, evergreens are bare of limbs as far up as they can browse. Here was a January bull using antlers to break off green twigs beyond the reach of his mouth, then eating what fell. Evergreens are not natural food for elk, but we are talking survival here.*

LEAVING IN A HURRY *Shannon and George were watching two herd bulls with harems on the Gibbon Meadows in Yellowstone. It was evening and three young bulls kept moving in on the big boys. This one had the audacity to run right up to a cow, and immediately had to flee with a furious six-point bull on his tail. George was behind a tree across the river, right where both zoomed by within ten feet. Lucky to get any shot at all. We saw this young bull two days later miles away, still trying the same tactics. He probably ended up the fall mating season as worn-out as if he'd had a harem, but with nothing to show for it. Just wait 'til next year!*

Right: **VERY UNUSUAL** *This sleek big cow had a horn. Doesn't happen too often. There was a smaller button on the other side and both growths still carried velvet, even though it was October. She was with a group of other cows being courted by bulls, and the lover boys seemed to pay no heed to her unique ornament.*

Below: **GIMME A LITTLE KISS** *All brides in the big-game world are basically gained by violence and male-on-male intimidation. But we've also observed time and time again, there seems to be more to animal romance than just whipping all rivals. Successful males practice many forms of romantic wooing, some of which we humans consider rather weird. We've often noticed touching gestures of affection. The females like to be courted a bit. Call such things courting rituals or whatever, it's nice.*

Above: **A BRASH INTRUDER** *The young bull (foreground) noticed luscious looking females in a big harem and started casually grazing in their direction, carefully avoiding any eye contact with the big guy. He's not foolin' the boss bull. The kid is about to get run right back in the woods. Can't blame a guy for tryin'.*

Right: **BAD HAIR DAY** *No wild animal looks too sharp when shedding its winter coat. This bull is no exception. Right now he just wants a lot of that new grass and a handy rubbin' tree. Bull elk and other ungulates don't wallow as much as buffalo, but they like a good roll now and then.*

NOT FOR REAL *A couple of young bulls know they have no chance against a herd bull this coming fall but they do dream and practice, practice, practice. Once in a while one of these younger guys gets lucky in love, but not very often. All of this has to do with the "survival of the fittest" theory, however, we've noticed "the pure old luck" theory sometimes carries the day.*

Left: MUTUAL FRIENDS
Everyone likes a good back scratch now and then, even those of us not pestered by ticks and flies. That's why this female elk is happy with the eight cowbirds scratching and picking around up there. She's probably telling that middle bird, "a little lower and to the right." Wildlife writer John Winnie told us these are cow birds. If they had been sitting on a male elk, maybe he'd have said they were bull birds. We'll ask him about that.

Right: **A SEVEN POINTER** We can't help thinking bull elk are glad when the fall loving season is over. Two weeks earlier this big male was fighting off homewreckers, chasing philandering wives, bugling every ten minutes and going without sleep or food. And the worst of it was the crazy mating game started way back in September. It is over now; Miss Wapiti Universe could stroll by and this bull wouldn't give her a glance. (Wapiti is an Indian word for elk.) Mother Nature knows when to turn off the heat. This bull is going to do nothing but eat and rest so he can get back that lost weight. (We call this guy a seven-pointer because out west we only count one side.)

Above: **GREAT ELK COUNTRY** *It's all here: towering mountains, protective open timber, and new grass coming through. A herd of elk is following the receding snow back to higher country where the bulls can shed their horns and the cows give birth to calves. There were eighteen wapiti in the herd, but only a few show in the photo. This spot is near Two Dog Flats on the eastern front of the Rockies in Glacier Park.*

Left: **ONE MORE MONTH** *It's the middle of February and the next month is the toughest. Stored body fat is gone, nutritional reserves are low, and food is scarce. Elk like this young bull wear trails from different yarding areas because breaking new ones takes precious energy. Took this shot in late afternoon after it had warmed up to only twenty-eight below zero. Most hooved animals in northern climes have hollow hair and other body defenses against cold temperatures that humans couldn't tolerate very long, let alone day after day.*

Right: **EATING A TREE** *The large fires of 1988 in Yellowstone killed millions of trees, and that wasn't all bad. Fire is a natural and necessary element in rebirth and growth. This big bull was in a burn area biting off the outside dead bark to get at the cambium layer underneath. Saw many of them doing this to stay alive. In the past we have seen downed aspen trees in the Lamar Valley with big sections of wood chewed out by hungry elk. There is a lot of government politics involved in wildlife management, too often unproductive and harmful. But this is not a political book. George worked in Washington, D.C., during the Kennedy administration on these matters and found it very frustrating.*

Left: **BIG BULL RESTING** *On Christmas day in 1996 we drove to the elk winter range on the south boundary of Glacier Park. El Niño was blamed for a near record snowfall that year. Before it was over, many wild animals perished. The good news is that biologists were heartened by the high percentage of animals that made it in spite of extra deep snows. Used a 600mm lens from U.S. Highway 2 to get this shot.*

Above: **DIGGING FOR GRASS** *Cows and calves were pawing for cured grass beneath the snow. Wintering grazers know where the least snow accumulates and yard up in such places. Nature's best plan for elk is migrating to lower lands, but with the coming of ranchers to lowlands, the normal winter ranges were claimed for cattle. Elk are not too welcome.*

The National Elk Foundation has been making great progress in acquiring winter ranges, trying to ease situations such as this. Elk leaving the southern part of Yellowstone Park along historic migration routes are artificially fed by the thousands at Jackson Hole, Wyoming. The Boy Scouts in Jackson Hole collect the shed antlers for a yearly auction. May be the wealthiest troop in America.

Left: **FANCY BED THERE** *Minerals deposited by geysers and underground springs of Yellowstone produce many beautiful formations. That's what America's first national park is all about. Elk likely don't care that this formation gleams like polished marble. They just like sacking out on it. That pretty couch is hard, but it's also quite warm. People are forbidden to even touch this stuff, let alone sleep there.*

Above: **PALS FOR NOW** *It is amazing the way so many big animal males are buddy-buddy most of the year and then engage in vicious fights during the fall for females. This phenomenon is true with many big prey species such as deer, elk and bighorn sheep. It is as if Mother Nature presses a button one day and they become enemies, then thirty to ninety days later another button is pressed and they're friends again. Seems to be a survival thing. These two big bull elk have not quite developed their new fighting antlers. It is July and a time for taking life easy. One may kill the other in September. If not, they'll be back here loafing together on Mission Creek next summer. Elk live longer than deer. We've heard of some reaching fifteen years and rumors of a few into their twenties.*

Right: **DOGGONE TICK** *Spotted calf elk has a little itchy in a touchy place to reach.*

GRIZZLY BEARS

A Griz Called "OJ"

When George got this photo of Grizzly Number 181, the bear already had a notorious past and was trying to stay out of trouble by catching cutthroat trout in a stream above Yellowstone Lake. Number 181 came to be called "OJ" by biologists because they found him to be "a great open field runner." When Ranger Shannon eventually saw this photo he asked, "Dad, how close were you for this shot? If I'd have seen you sneaking around up there I might have had to issue you a citation." Still, he had to agree that it was a good picture. I told him I was up in a perfect tree with my bear spray and was using a 300-millimeter telephoto lens. In the fifteen minutes I was watching OJ he caught two cutthroat trout and devoured them completely, bones and all, "just like a Norwegian eatin' sardines."

When first seen by rangers in 1989, OJ was a good-sized cub still traveling with his mother and sister. The female cub had been partially paralyzed from a spinal bite by another bear, and dismayed tourists saw her dragging her rear legs, trying to keep up with the family. She did not live long. Later the mother was trapped and moved back into the wilderness, but she returned to Yellowstone Lake the next year. She was considered a threat to humans, and just before she was to be "put down," a zoo in San Antonio, Texas, agreed to take her.

Meanwhile, in April 1990, OJ was trapped and moved to Slough Creek where he stayed out of trouble until August. Then he made regional headlines by raiding the Teddy Roosevelt Riders' barbecue. It was the end of the famous annual trail ride. People had come from all points of the planet to honor our great conservationist President with a wilderness experience to end all wilderness experiences. The outdoor adventure was to finish off with refreshments and an unforgettable feast served and eaten in God's country. Chefs were busy beneath the trees at Yancy's Hole, near Tower Junction, preparing to grill ten dozen thick steaks while the Trail Riders cleared the dust from their throats.

Alas! One of God's furry children decided to crash the party. Cooks and servers fled the scene while anywhere from fifty to one hundred pounds of steak were consumed by OJ, the fast-growing grizzly. He topped off the steaks with a few bowls of potato salad, plus corn on the cob for dessert. It was the greatest day in OJ's life, but there was a price to pay. He was trapped again. I never found out if they used the remaining potato salad as bait or not.

OJ gained a radio collar around his neck and was moved to a remote area. Shortly after our photo was taken in June 1991, the young griz began showing up around the tourist spots, where he had to settle for a few unguarded burgers, french fries, and candy bars. He was again caught and moved, this time to Yonce Peak, but he certainly knew there were better places to eat than on that remote mountain. As the song goes, "How you gonna keep 'em down on the farm, after they've seen Paree?" OJ made the fifty tough miles back to Grant Village in nine days.

Biologists had already given OJ more opportunities to reform than most troublesome bears get, but since he had never shown aggression toward humans they gave him one more chance to go straight. This time they moved him to a very remote Wyoming wilderness at Crescent Mountain, south of Yellowstone. He was observed there several times and seemed to be doing okay, but in September his radio collar went dead. After that there was no way to locate him.

Human tragedy played a role in this grizzly bear tale. Two wildlife biologists were killed in a plane crash while trying to locate OJ's radio signals.

OJ may have been shot by a poacher and his collar dismantled. No one knows for sure what happened to him. Considering his luck in the past, we like to think Number 181 is still roaming the Teton Wilderness, hoping for one more rendezvous with the Teddy Roosevelt Riders...preferably around dinner time.

A note: finding qualified homes for grizzlies with people problems is very difficult. Several bears have to be destroyed each year in Montana, Alaska, and Wyoming for that reason. Grizzly biologists say the bears reproduce well in captivity, so wildlife parks and zoos are content to maintain their own supply rather than take in rogues from the wild. Several years ago, the Montana Fish and Game Department sent queries to every state in the Union asking them to take a few surplus grizzlies. The only state to give an affirmative reply was Alaska. Its fish and game officials said they would take any extra grizzlies Montana sent, providing they could exchange them for wolves on a pound-for-pound basis.

have to either give captured animals a number, or name them after a lawyer to avoid emotional attachment.

George Washington was tranquilized so he could be measured, eartagged and equipped with a radio tracking collar. Unlike some grizzlies in the northern U.S. Rockies, George avoided getting into trouble with people all his life and spent his last few years in that same area. A different griz name Old Giefer tore up over thirty cabins in the Glacier Park border areas, including two of ours a hundred miles apart. Giefer's downfall was an addiction to strawberry jam. Beat anything he could find in the woods. He was trapped and moved into wilderness

A GRIZ NAMED GEORGE *Back in the summer of 1981, researchers still gave names to tagged animals. They snared this big one near our remote cabins in the North Fork of the Flathead. It was July Fourth, so to honor the elder Ostrom along with our first president, he was named George Washington. Nowadays, the government wildlife biologists*

areas twice, but returned for a little more jam. At our North Fork lodge, he didn't tear up anything inside but did make kindling out of the front and back doors. He never learned about using knobs. The following spring he was legally shot by a trophy hunter in Canada about twenty miles northwest of this spot.

STARTING OVER *A few female griz do not get very big, like this one. Against great odds, George ran into her in the wilds twice. The first time she had a cub, and it was touch and go for a minute. Biologists have to use numbers for bears, but we call this one Tillie. She came out the west side of Glacier Park in the spring of 1995 with two cubs. One cub was killed on the railroad tracks, and she and the other cub were trapped and taken into the high country. That is where George and the Over-the-Hill-Gang ran into them that fall. Tillie was also suspect in the bad mauling of a hiker in the spring of '96, but may have been innocent. Got this photo in early spring of 1997. She had no cubs that year. May have sworn off.*

FIGHTING FOR FUN *Grizzlies must fight in the wild for mates, for food, and for territory. They start training within days of coming out of the den with their mothers. Because they have few natural enemies, they mainly fight other bears, playfully as in this photo, or for real. Nature's rule seems to be, "The bigger the predator the longer it lives and the fewer of them there are." Wardens tracked a female grizzly in Montana's Cabinet Mountains that lived beyond 30 years.*

While grizzlies can instantly turn into one of the most formidable beasts on earth, they also do a lot of goofing off. We've seen them sliding down grassy slopes, playing tag, throwing things in the air and catching them. They love rollicking in the water. Grizzlies at the Olympic Game Farm learned to throw rocks and hard clay at passing people and cars. Put a dent in our 1984 station wagon.

As a reporter, George has gone to all ten sites where people have been killed by grizzlies in Glacier Park from 1967 to May 1998, and has interviewed a dozen mauling victims. Shannon has had many adventures with the big bears, both as a ranger protecting tourists from bear situations and as a private person enjoying the wilds. We believe in giving them a wide berth and carrying a quality pepper spray in case things go bad in the back country.

PLUMB DISGUSTED *Millions of visitors come to Yellowstone Park each summer, but this guy is leaving...had it "right up to here." He can't stand another day of tour buses, knobby-kneed New Yorkers, bear jams or government biologists. The big silvertip male wants peace and quiet. Problem is, this road leads to Cody, Wyoming, and that town is not known for being too quiet. Maybe he's figuring on heading for the nearby Absaroka Wilderness until things calm down in the winter and he can return to hibernate through the snowmobile invasion.*

RASCAL CUB *George watched this Glacier Park grizzly mother for hours and wondered why she didn't spank that lightest colored cub. Fall was coming and they were supposed to be looking for berries and roots, but one mostly just raised whoopee. Was constantly sneaking up and attacking his sister or his mother, boxing with the bushes, throwing sticks, climbing little trees 'til they bent over. Even rolled a rock down on his loved ones. All little animals need play time, but this one was making it a career. Female bears do swat their cubs, but it's usually in serious situations, like when she wants them up a tree...right now.*

UNFLAPPABLE GRIZ *Thousands of visitors to Glacier Park hike from Logan Pass across the Hanging Gardens to Hidden Lake Overlook on the Continental Divide each summer. To save the fragile tundra, there is a unique boardwalk, and managers discourage grizzlies from hanging around there. This big silvertip showed up in the summer of 1997 to feed on roots and berries. Rangers waited all day until he entered the "no no zone," seventy-five yards from the walk. Four biologists charged him with barking Russian bear dogs while firing explosive shotgun charges near him. Surprised by all the attention, he stood up to appraise the "charge of the fright brigade," then turned and raced away over a knoll. The biologists left the area. George ran back up the boardwalk beyond the knoll see if the bear went over the mountain, but found he'd only gone two hundred yards, stopped, and was calmly digging roots as if he'd never been frightened in his life.*

Above: **A STALK IN THE PARK** *Four of us went to Mt. Henkel to photograph these rams one spring and ended up watching them stalked for an hour by two grizzlies. This photo was taken just before the bears came along. There were a total of twenty-six rams in this group and not one was lying in a way to make direct eye contact with another. That is just not done in better bighorn circles.*

Right: The big female grizzly and her two-year-old cub first tried approaching from below the sheep and cross-wind, but the rams saw them. The bears then circled downwind and tried a little sneak. In this shot the griz realize that the wind advantage is useless because the lookout rams have them clearly in view. Unless a mature sheep, elk or deer is sick or injured, a grizzly has to be very, very close to have any chance for a catch. A grizzly is fast, but not that fast.

At this point, the big bear resorted to a dirty, sneaky trick; walked nonchalantly up the hill to the left of this photo in clear view, acting like the last thing in this world she wanted for supper was a bighorn sheep. Completely ignored the rams she knew were watching—never looked back—and worked her way to the top of the small ridge and casually disappeared. George was fooled. He said, "Well, that little deal is over. Let's go on up the cliffs and see if we can find some goats."

Twenty minutes later we were on a cliff ledge and looked below at the sheep. Son-in-law Scott Duncan exclaimed, "Can you believe that? Those grizzlies are in the gulch coming back in a hurry. They're out of sight of the sheep."

The mother bear was in the lead and they stayed hidden in the gully until she knew from the wind they were directly east of the rams. It was now or never. Up out of the gulch they came.

(continued on page 30...)

(continued from page 28…)

Above: The distance from the sheep was too far to make an attack. She knew it instantly and stopped. Had there been a ram close to the rim of the gulch she might have had a small chance. She stood there disappointed for a minute and told the cub to forget it. It was interesting to notice that all during the deadly game a few big rams kept watch for the bears and the rest went on eating, resting and chewing their cuds.

Left: All the work in trying to stalk and fool the rams had the grizzlies overheated. They have the same cooling system as a dog, panting. That's not enough when they're still in winter coats and it's a warm day. They went to a snow bank and rolled around in it then snuggled in for a cooling rest. Our gang stayed up in the cliffs above, trying for photos but not getting close. Shannon took this with a 300mm lens. The mother never took her eyes off us. That's a little spooky.

GEORGE FINDS A SCARY SIGN *You'd look a little spooked yourself if you saw this kind of claw marks on a tree in the wilderness. Even though these are not too high, the bear that made them had a mighty big paw. We've seen scratch marks higher up than a man can reach. That's really scary. Bears do this as a warning to other bears—and probably to nosy people.*

NOT ALONE *Once in a while, people in the wilds will see a bear cub that appears to be alone. Never believe it. Never approach it. The quickest way to trigger an attack from a female grizzly or black is to pose a real or imagined threat to its young. A lengthy study of bears by Dr. Charles Jonkel revealed that cub mortality is very low in the two or three years they are with their mothers, even though older males often try to kill cubs not theirs. The mother's defense is unbelievably furious. We have been "bluff charged" a few times and the mother's speed is scary. If you get between the cubs and mother, there is no bluff to it.*

MUTINY IN THE RANKS *Shannon watched these bears in Yellowstone. Mother griz wants to go up the hill to deeper timber and one cub is ready to do that, but the other one? It wants to stay right here close to the creek. It's hard to tell at this distance; however, we think the facial expression and the body language say, "I ain't goin'."*

WORK HAZARDS *It was often an adventure for Shannon just making the short walk from his quarters out to Yellowstone's East Gate entrance station. In his five years there, he met many wandering wild things. Bison were common. The worst were grizzly bears...in the dark. Late one night, another ranger phoned from the cabin area to Shan at the gate. Said they had just run a grizzly off the porch and it was "west of the entrance." Shan stepped out to look and ran into the bear, but was able to get back inside and slam the door. He called the cabin and asked, "Howcum you said west of the entrance?" and the reply was, "I said next to the entrance."*

Shan got to recognizing many of the bears in that area and followed their fortunes. A female with three cubs had to be captured after getting into a shed outside the park and killing some puppies. Two of those cubs may still be at the Seattle Zoo. An adult male was shot after it destroyed a small, privately owned apple orchard. Grizzlies do not pick one apple at a time. They tear down the tree and eat 'em all.

Female #104 was best known for producing cubs and causing bear jams on the road to Sylvan Pass for many years, but she never bothered humans or property. She had a "runt" cub one year, which was killed by a car, and a larger male of that litter was shipped to a zoo. #104 showed up again in 1995 with a single new cub and it was one of those super playful models. One of #104's older daughters was also around in '95 with cubs of her own. She seemed to follow her mother through the mountains, but Shannon never saw them closer to each other than 300 yards.

HE ISN'T DEAD *Most pictures you see of a grizzly in this pose are ones shot by either a hunter or a game management warden. Not this guy. He is alive and wild, but a little pooped. Shan spotted this big male while fishing the South Fork of the Shoshone River and was very careful not to wake him up.*

Above: **GRIZZLY BEAR BOTTOM** *There was only one safe way to get a photo from this close. Shannon did not take it in the wild. We include it to show how short a bear's tail is, and to show bears have a sole.*

Above right: **DON'T TRUST HIM** *A captive grizzly, almost two years old, and still playing "This little piggy went to market."*

Right: **SNORING** *Had to visit the Olympic Game Farm (at Sequim, Washington, on the Olympic Peninsula) to get close enough to see if a grizzly snores. This one did...but not as bad as some guys we've gone camping with.*

PLUMB DISAPPOINTED *There are few things so frustrating as peeling all the bark off a fallen tree and not finding any fat worms to eat. This grizzly just can't believe it. He hasn't learned yet, you have to work on logs that have started to decay.*

Above: **FROSTED FEMALE** *The sun is helping this cow shed frost her coat gathered during the night. Notice the rime is heavier on the shady side.*

Right: **WORKING DOWNHILL** *Yes, an old bull is working his way through deep snow toward lower country near West Yellowstone. Coming in that morning we met several such animals using the packed snowmobile trail to seek grass outside the park. A few private citizens near the boundary have fed hay to such animals in the past, while others immediately call authorities and demand removal. At least one man fed elk but shot bison because, "They tear up everything." It is a complex problem for all involved, including the animals.*

BUFFALO

Eating Bison Religiously

Little George started first grade in the fall of 1934 in a two-room school on the Flathead Indian Reservation in Montana. Enrollment was about half Native Americans and half white settler kids. I was excited to start learning the Three Rs, and my mother was pleased that the government furnished a hot noon meal, so she didn't have to make me a lunch.

Turned out the hot meal was "surplus buffalo" from the National Bison Range. Local ladies were paid to prepare it each day, and I recall they didn't have far-reaching imaginations. Monday started off with big roasts that became reheated roast on Tuesday, followed by oven-warmed buffalo sandwiches Wednesday, buffalo stew Thursday, and ground buffalo hash on Friday. We kids figured the Bison Range was butchering the toughest, oldest bulls, because there couldn't be road-kill out there in the hills. That menu started getting to me but it was during the depression and I knew grocery money was tight for everybody, so I didn't complain.

Didn't take me too long to realize that each Friday, Jimmy Pelly got macaroni and cheese. When no one was around, I asked Jimmy howcum he didn't have to eat buffalo on Friday. Said he was a Catholic and Catholics couldn't eat meat that day. Sure enough, by the next Friday I had turned into a Catholic. Couldn't spell it, had no idea what it meant, but I was one and let the servers know.

Trouble was, one of the cooks was Mrs. Busybody, who lived across the road from us, and she couldn't wait to inform my mother, "George was telling lies at school today." Mom was waiting when I got home and said if I was willing to stay a Methodist, she'd fix me a lunch for Friday and any other day.

I was a Catholic only for one day, but it was a fine macaroni and cheese day.

BEEN TO BATTLE *Unlike Beau Brummel (see page 43), here's a regular-type rutting bull—just a mess. He didn't seem to have one cow to call his own, but looked like he'd fought every other bull on the range four times. A half hour after we took this shot he tried one more time to win a wife and came out looking even worse. If things didn't get better, he may have sworn off women.*

Left: **JUST BORN** *Momma buffalo is licking her brand new calf to get the circulation going and make him presentable to the group. Unlike deer, bighorns and antelope, bison don't mind having young with the herd around. We've seen them born in a crowd.*

Below: **INTO THE CURRENT** *The grass must be greener on the other side or else bison wouldn't cross rivers so much. When buffalo covered the Great Plains, huge herds swam even the widest rivers, such as the Missouri. It isn't easy going for young calves. These are a few months old, and seem to do well by swimming in the wake of the older animals. An old horn hunter we know has found the skulls and bones of many bison, including big bulls, in what were once well used crossings on the Milk River. There are no more of those giant spring migrations, so drowning isn't a big threat to present-day animals.*

SERIOUS BUSINESS *It's plain to see buffalo cows are not thrilled or excited about males fighting over them. They're still busy taking care of last spring's little bundle of joy. Bison bulls are sometimes fatally gored in the mating season battles, or badly injured. The most heated duels take place during a three- to four-day period at the onset of rut. Other fights occur afterwards, but the dominant bulls are quickly established. National Bison Range foreman "Babe" May told us the occasional fatal fights happen when four-year-old bulls use their agility to outmaneuver the older males, especially when they get uphill of their adversary and use gravity to offset the weight difference. Wounds are inflicted by hooking horns into the sides of the opponent.*

LEARNING THE FACTS OF LIFE

Watched this big bull raising a ruckus in a large herd along the Yellowstone River. He was really on the fight and looking for love. Everywhere he went, the young male calf stuck right with him. There are role models in all species.

EXPLORING *This buffalo calf is almost a day old and figures it is time to start making a few friends, but she won't stray far from the mother. The umbilical cord has dried. We read some place that when first born, buffalo calves don't have a hump. This one looks a tad humpy to us.*

BEAUTIFUL PLACE TO WALLOW *The dictionary says wallowing means to "relax, roll about in water, mud, or dust, indulge immoderately—roll heavily and clumsily." Next to eating, wallowing is a buffalo's favorite sport. Calves think it's fun. Old bulls do it constantly. American bison have been wallowing here for thousands of years. That one hole down there is bigger than a house. It is on the high plains next to the eastern front of the Rockies. The American bison, i.e. buffalo, were wiped out in this area near Waterton, British Columbia, in the late 1880s, but they are back now.*

Left: **BIG MEDICINE** *Not quite pure albino was this large bull born on the National Bison Range at Moiese, Montana, before World War II. He attracted thousands of sightseers during his lifetime and lived to an old age for bison, twenty-six. His whiteness was not complete because of brown hair between his horns. He did father a pure albino calf, which was taken to the National Zoo in Washington, D.C., but it was carelessly fed a bale of hay containing pieces of sharp wire, which killed it. When Big Medicine died, he was preserved by artist Bob Scriver, and you can now see the mounted specimen at the Montana State Historical Society museum in Helena.*

Native American oral history contains stories about the religious significance of albino bison, and modern Indian people still honor the occasional white buffalo. Ted Turner and Jane Fonda have one of the largest bison herds on earth, in southeastern Montana. Maybe one of these days an albino will show up in the Turner herds, because the genes of Big Medicine are represented there.

Right: **BISON ROUNDUP**
Every fall brings a roundup on the National Bison Range at Moiese, Montana. Up to five hundred animals are run through corrals and get shots if needed, then surplus animals are sold at auction. That keeps the herd in balance with the carrying capacity of the range and pays the bills. This photo shows long time range foreman "Babe" May helping bring in a herd. Sitting on a hill watching, it sounded more like they were herding African lions. A disturbed buffalo herd produces a voluminous roaring like nothing we've ever listened to.

MAGNIFICENT SPECIMEN *This "herd bull" weighs well over two thousand pounds and the cow about half of that. Mystery to us was how other bulls in the area were frazzled, muddy, their hair matted, or horns splintered, but this guy didn't have a hair out of place. We named him Beau Brummel. He whispered sweet nothings in the lady's ear and she followed him everywhere.*

THE PREDATORS WAIT *Coyotes, wolves and other hungry hunters and scavengers are a constant presence near wintering game herds, in national parks, on private lands, national forests and high plains. It has been that way for millions of years.*

FORTY-TWO BELOW ZERO
Shannon and Mike Schlegel used cross country skis to reach these bison near Old Faithful in Yellowstone. The sun was just rising near a steaming hot pool that kept snow melted, but the mist has frozen on a cow and calf. Extreme cold is something bison can withstand; availability of food determines whether they survive or not. In the long winter of 1996-97, hundreds of buffalo perished of malnutrition inside Yellowstone and 400 more were shot after migrating out of the park. Concern is that some bison carry brucellosis, which may infect domestic cattle. Taxpayer estimates indicate 800 government bureaus were working on the problem in 1998.

SHARING TOUGH TIMES *Many bison and bull elk winter near the Firehole River. We've not noticed any aggression between the two species over scarce feed. In late winter the name of the game is "save energy."*

A LONER *'Tis a solitary life for old buffalo bulls. When the day comes they can no longer compete for cows, they start drifting away from the herds. Sometimes two or three will roam together, but many seem to turn their backs on all company, spending long years in solitude. Their social life is zilch.*

BUFFALO IN MAY *Long cold nights and digging through snow are gone now. Calves are being born, and it's time to wallow and eat flowers. Visitors can drive through Alexander Basin on the National Bison Range, but they shouldn't leave their cars. In Yellowstone National Park every summer, several tourists get too close to these shaggy critters and wind up in the hospital or worse.*

HOW TO WALLOW: *Never wallow on a steep place. If there isn't an old wallow handy, start a new one. Lying on your side, start rocking back and forth, scooching to and fro and kicking. After getting that side well wallowed, try to roll up on the backbone with all four feet in the air, wiggle a bit then fall over on the unwallowed side and repeat the rolling, rocking, scooching and kicking. When well wallowed, get back on feet to shimmy and shake entire hide until all dead bugs, loose hair and dust blow away.*

COMING THROUGH THE GATE *Buffalo cannot be casually driven along like your average milk cow. Multiple horsemen at the Moiese roundup have become skilled at separating small groups of ten to fifteen animals from bigger herds and driving them into the corrals. It has to be swiftly carried out at full gallop or the group cuts back to the main herd. It is hazardous work requiring buffalo savvy and the best horses. No place for a green-horn cowboy. After making this shot from behind a post, George decided to find a spot a little farther from the action. Added to flying dust, pounding hooves, bellowing and shaking ground, this sight charging into the camera lens was more startling than anticipated. He thought he was a goner.*

Above: **INTERESTING HAIR STYLE?** *Some males of every species will do weird things to get attention. Bison are no different. This bull is showing off to the cows and signaling rivals, "I'm one tough dude." When mature bulls start this kind of stuff, it means the mating season has arrived in buffalo country. Because buffalo cows carry calves longer than most ungulates, the rutting season comes in late summer rather than fall. We didn't stay around long enough to learn if "the green bush in the hair act" worked, but we hope so.*

Right: **HELPING AN ORPHAN**
This two-month-old buffalo was found alone and starving on the National Bison Range in June of 1972. Foreman Vic May told us the calf had been abandoned by its mother, a not uncommon thing, especially when it is her first. In this case there was a happy ending because a range rider brought in the hungry baby and taught it to drink domestic cow's milk from a nippled bottle. Young Shannon, his kid brother Clark, and their friend Joe Biby took turns serving lunch.

SUMMER CHALLENGE *This trio of young bighorn rams were acting cocky with each other. We watched them do the preliminary threat rituals and speculated as to who was going to bang heads with whom. Zoomed the lens in and caught all three in the pre-slam stance, standing on back legs to get more force. It was the last frame on the film, so we didn't get the crash. Normal fighting is done one-on-one, but these rams broke the rules of ethical head-butting. Lucky one didn't get hurt with the bad-angle attacks. It happens.*

BIGHORN SHEEP

A Real Buttinsky

As with all wildlife, we know some strange tales about bighorn sheep. They are butters. The little kids butt, the ewes butt, and the rams seem to live for seeing how hard they can slam into something headfirst. Most of the time this particular sheep habit doesn't bother humans, but a family living in the Cabinet Mountains of western Montana has a legitimate complaint about the practice.

The man of the house called me one day at my Kalispell radio station and started talking so fast I had a hard time getting details. When he slowed down a bit, I asked, "Now, as I understand it, you live at Bull Lake and have a wild bighorn sheep inside your house?"

"Yes. That is the exact situation."

"Please talk slowly and clearly because I want to take notes. Now tell me what happened."

"Well, I don't know how loud I should talk because the dang thing is eyeing me from the hallway."

"Did it sneak in through an open door?"

"No. It came to our picture window on the uphill side of the house and apparently saw its reflection. I noticed it making threatening gestures, but because I was inside all I could see was a bighorn sheep giving me a bad time. After the reflection apparently made threatening gestures back at the real sheep outside, that fool thing reared up on its hind legs and charged right through a double-thick thermopane into our living room. It is a big mess in here and those windows are not cheap, you know. Oh oh! It is snooping toward the kitchen."

"It was thoughtful of you to call our radio station. What are you going to do now?"

"I have phoned the game warden and he'll be here pretty soon. Called my neighbor and he said I should call you because you like stuff like this on your news. Glad my wife is in town getting groceries. She'd be scared half to death. Oh! Oh! It looks like that thing is headed for the bathroom. I don't know why sheep don't stay up in the mountains where they belong."

I took the man's phone number and said I'd call back if I thought of anything. I came up with the idea of having him hold a mirror in front of the sheep and then backing up toward an open door, but realized the ram might charge before he could duck aside. Unless the poor guy had some toreador training, he might end up with busted ribs or, at best, a broken mirror. Either way would be bad luck.

An hour later I called to learn that the sheep was headed for the hills. The man said his basement was one of those daylight models. He and the game warden had managed to herd the confused bighorn down the stairs and out the sliding glass doors. "Well, I'm certainly glad your problem is solved," I told him. "Has the game warden left yet?"

"Absolutely not. With the evidence gone, he knows there is no way I'll let him leave without helping to explain this mess to my wife when she gets home."

NO PLACE FOR A SISSY *Climbed up Mount Henkle through bitter cold to see how the bighorns were doing. Four rams came up over that snow cornice at the left and fought their way to bare ground, then lay down to rest. The Continental Divide of the Rockies is the skyline, with Mount Wilbur on the right.*

Took a couple of quick shots of the rams and left without disturbing their rest. They spend the whole winter up here and rely on the constant winds to clear exposed ridges where they feed. In his great book, High Life, *John Winnie has photos of sheep with frosted eyelids. John frosted more than that. Wild sheep seem to have more trouble from outbreaks of disease than from the elements. They are tough.*

OLD PINK NOSE *In the seventies, this big fellow was absolute boss when late fall came to Henkle and Altyn mountains in Glacier Park. He was getting well up in bighorn years when we took this last shot of him in 1972. He'd come through the rut in good shape and probably had more good years ahead. Rams' horns keep growing all their lives and many fellows get well up into their teens. This one had a small scar on his nose that was a bright pink and that's one of the ways we could recognize him. In the few fights we saw him in, the other ram didn't last long. One good slam from Pink Nose sent most contenders straight to the showers.*

VERY, VERY UNUSUAL *These skulls with weathered horns were found on the National Bison Range many years ago. The foreman, "Babe" May, told us the big rams were fighting on a steep side hill in a timbered area and apparently slammed together then shoved or slid under a downed log. They were pinned underneath it in such a way neither could get free. Locked heads are fairly common in antlered animals, but this is the only incident we know happening to bighorns.*

Above: **PRECOCIOUS LAMB?** *Don't know what that yearling bighorn has going for him, but he is acting right at home with a band of big rams. Rather unusual. Maybe that's his grandpa there. One- and two-year-old males normally hang out in little groups of their own, not far from where the females and the new spring lambs find secluded alpine summer pasture. Males and females of this high-living species go to different places for the hotter months, then rendezvous in the fall. Conversely, we've sometimes seen two-year-old rams sticking with their mothers' bands. Maybe some are just harder to wean.*

Left: **FAULTY HORN** *That horn must have been damaged early on. It didn't seem to interfere with the ewe's ability to graze; however, she may be using her handicap to generate sympathy from tourists on the Many Glacier road in Glacier Park. We believe we observed this same sheep a year later with a lamb, so she did find romance. In one incident there was a dead sheep by the road and an autopsy showed she had been given a bag of chips. Eating a salty plastic sack had killed her. "Do Not Feed the Animals."*

OKAY! TAKE THAT *Once they get enough spring food in their bellies to feel good, the young bighorn rams spend a lot of time slam whamming each other around. A bit like hockey players, they even fight to see who gets to fight next.*

Left: **COPTER CAPTURE** *We mention elsewhere the ongoing transplant program to help bighorn sheep re-establish in areas where they were hunted out years ago. This is one of the ways.*

Bighorns do well on Wild Horse Island in Flathead Lake, Montana, but they overproduce for available food so the surplus is used to start herds in other places and to replenish gene pools of existing populations. A fellow from Australia developed a unique way of catching wild animals by flying above with that powerful little copter and shooting a net over 'em. Then a guy—probably related to Crocodile Dundee—leaps out and ties their legs with straps and blindfolds them. A rope is fastened to the straps and the captured animals are quickly airlifted upside down to a field lab for blood tests, tagging and truck transport.

These guys work fast, and several of the trips took only twenty minutes from takeoff to capture and back. Biologists say this method reduces trauma on the animals because they aren't chased far or shot with tranquilizer darts. We told the Dundee guy we wanted to go along for pictures if he tried this on grizzly bears. He said it might be a year or two.

Below: **TOURING PUG** *Here's a relatively young ram with a nice curl, but he's already chipped up the horns and got a mouse over one eye. We saw him in Banff National Park, Alberta, and the bigger old ram he'd just fought had a broken leg. Mating battles sometimes leave winners and losers alike with injuries that make them easier victims for big predators, because all beasts alike must deal with deep snows and the frigid days of winter soon to follow.*

LIVING STATUE

Before summer tourists arrive at the magnificent Many Glacier Hotel in Glacier Park, bighorn sheep come down from the peaks to check things out. This two-year-old ram ignored several signs asking visitors to not climb on the rock railing. When he saw us photographing his transgressions, he turned into a statue. They'll do that, you know.

Left: **FIRST OUTING** *The little guy was born a couple of days ago on a cliff ledge. Mother has come down to eat, but he's not ready yet to meet her band. An amazing thing happened. There were two other ewes grazing there with new ones. Returning to the safe cliffs, they had to cross a swift rushing stream four feet wide. The first two ewes leaped over and their lambs followed, but this little guy balked. He told his mother it was too far. She came back and took him farther up where the stream was split and he only had to make two little jumps. It was a moving moment for George and young son Shannon in the spring of 1973.*

Below: **ARE WE LOST, MA?** *Even the newest bighorn kids are taught to make their way down and up treacherous cliffs, because cliffs are their friends. Prime rams can run at top speed down and up such places. When these two are grown, they'll think this is easy street. Many times we've watched rams drop hundreds of feet off almost perpendicular cliffs, just touching here and there to control direction. Might call it "extreme" cliff descending. Powerful legs are a must.*

Above: **THE DAY CARE CENTER** *After the kids are about ten days old their mothers rejoin the band. This is a typical bighorn day care center. Four kids were behaving themselves fairly well, but two others kept wandering off to sniff balsamroot flowers. Besides not getting in the class picture, they probably missed their naps and were fussy all afternoon. Ewes without kids of their own often volunteer for day care duty and the mothers also take turns.*

Right: **MOVING DAY** *Tomorrow this healthy four-year-old ram will be on a new range hundreds of miles away, starting another herd of bighorns. Right now he's unhappy with the blindfold, but he's more manageable that way while undergoing a physical. We'd bet the next time a copter comes over he'll hide under the nearest tree.*

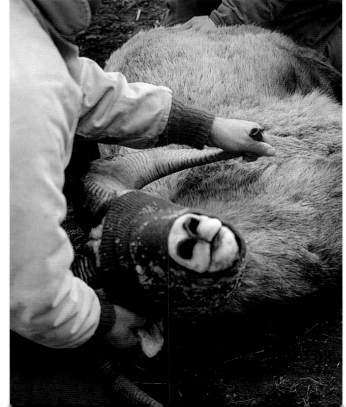

59

HIGH COUNTRY LADIES

While the young males are hitting heads together and their mothers having babies, the one- and two-year-old ewes form little cliques and concentrate on girl things, like eating. These were on Dawson Pass of the Continental Divide. Good scenery up there.

FULL CURL RAM *When bighorns get to be five or six years old they are serious contenders in the fall fights for ewes. This guy is in that group and, from the chips in his horns, he's been in a few serious fights already. Right now it is summer and he's eating himself into good shape for the coming battles. There are minor scuffles year around, but those involve social status and turf. During the last twenty-five years, bighorn sheep in the West have made a tremendous comeback in numbers because hunters' license and tax money has been used in re-establishing old ranges and for live transplanting.*

LOOKING FOR TROUBLE *These rams are big, the kind that win most battles for turf or ewes. Just as in boxing, the toughest battles occur when the contestants are evenly matched. After slamming horns together, both are dazed for a minute and sometimes stand like this trying to get their eyes uncrossed. Besides the great curling horns, bighorn males have a highly developed cushion of porous bone on the frontal skull, which absorbs shock. The "whack" of two this size slamming together can be heard a long ways.*

A MIGHTY BIG DOG *They say all domestic dogs descended from wolves, but it is difficult picturing the neighbor's poodle being related to something this big. Researchers tracking radio-collared wolves on the west side of Glacier observed wolf packs on two occasions attacking grizzly bears.*

The man who designed the Wyoming license plate spent over twenty-five years in the early 1900s as a paid government wolf hunter. His name was George Ostrom—no relation to us—and we made friends with him when he was a very active one hundred years old. Said he hated wolves when he first took the job but came to respect them, and eventually got to liking them. They are a complex, beautiful animal.

THE CAMAS WOLF PACK *How many wolves are in this meadow? We were too busy trying to shoot pictures from a bumpy airplane to make an accurate count, but studying this picture we see at least two white ones and four blacks. They were located by telemetry (radio collars). The pack had eaten their fill from an elk they brought down and were basking in the late August sunshine. They were so used to being observed from aircraft they paid no attention as we circled, cut the engine and glided over them. See any looking up?*

This group of wolves grew from individual animals coming into the United States from Canada and have re-established a strong presence in Glacier Park and the Flathead National Forest, Montana. Diane Boyd, the "Wolf Lady," stayed at our Moose City cabins for many years, live-trapping, studying and tracking these magnificent predators under a recovery and research program directed by the University of Montana. Students often came to help. Several other northern Montana packs have been formed by spinoffs from this group, and at least twice in recent years the Camas pack attacked and killed leaders of another pack intruding into territory they claim.

In the early decades of this century, the big carnivores (meat eaters) such as wolves, grizzly bears and lions were almost wiped out by private and paid government hunters, even in the National Parks. George remembers many families augmenting their incomes during the Depression by bounty hunting. Lions were worth twenty dollars. In the 1980s and '90s, the predators rebounded but not without great expense and many emotional political battles. The biggest fights were over the transplanting of Canadian wolves into Yellowstone Park and the central Idaho wilderness.

WOLVES

OCTOBER'S PUPPY *By late fall, the spring wolf pups can get close to adult size, especially their feet. Wolves are shy and, whether you see them in the wild or at a game farm, this is usually all you get, peaking from the trees.*

Left: **CAPTURED CATTLE RUSTLER** *The Lost Prairie wolf pack got into trouble in 1988 when they started killing cattle instead of deer. Several were shot, including the big male leader, but the female, two pups and a grandpa were caught alive and transplanted. This is the female. She left the big pups and traveled hundreds of miles across mountain ranges, rivers and lakes before finding another male west of Missoula, Montana, and forming a new family, the Nine Mile Pack. At least two books have been written about that group. Her first pups did not survive in Glacier Park and the old male with them was shot in a herd of cattle near the boundary.*

Below: **TWO GRAY WOLVES** *The whole pack helps raise wolf puppies produced by an alpha male and female. Litters are usually born in April and are ready to start learning serious hunting by the following winter. These large canines are fairly adaptable and we observed a pack in northern British Columbia that survived by scavenging the ocean beaches. Gray wolves can be any color from white to brown, gray, or pure black. Real, honest-to-gosh, wild wolves are very hard to photograph in the wilderness. That's why we used this photo from a "controlled environment."*

Wolves are big. We know of no incident where a wild American or Canadian wolf has killed a human. There is one documented case of a wolf attack on a Canadian railroad worker many years ago, in which the animal was found to be rabid and was destroyed before injuring anyone.

COYOTES

WAITING FOR A TRAIN *Coyotes usually winter well. The little canids are opportunistic and have discovered rail lines are good hangouts because many game animals are hit by trains. This is one of many we've watched in huge Jasper National Park, Canada. A railroad runs completely through the park east and west. One time we were awakened in our Jasper motel by coyotes howling from Main Street. Sounded like they were on the doorstep.*

CURIOUS COYOTE PUPS *Horse wranglers told George and youngest son Clark a female coyote was hunting with her pups on Cracker Flats in Glacier Park, so we walked two miles up the trail and sat on a knoll. After a while we decided to make the "dying rabbit screech" by stretching a blade of grass between our thumbs and blowing short blasts. It worked. Across the flats came a female with four pups, running right at us. She would leap into the air to look over the brush. At about a hundred feet she spotted us, gave warning yaps to the pups and veered across a creek. One pup went with her, but three still wanted some rabbit. The mother kept frantically barking and one of these joined her but the last two stayed for several minutes. Doing anything to disturb or attract wild animals is now against national park rules, but it was legal then.*

SAGE BRUSH PROWLER

Spring means puppies in a den, new mouths to feed for adult coyotes. Saw one catching mice and burrowing gophers. The coyote springs high in the air, stares at the ground, listens very intently, then suddenly pounces. This one caught three gophers in fifteen minutes. Hunting in packs, coyotes pull off very complex plans to take down bigger prey or enemies. We remember a coyote howling from the hill near Grandma's ranch, taunting the watchdog. When the dog chased the coyote over the hill, he never came back because the whole pack was lying in ambush. They don't eat dogs, just don't want them around guarding lambs and hen houses.

WAITING PATIENTLY *Coyotes like to follow buffalo herds waiting for one to get hurt, sick, or die. Until that happens, they catch mice, gophers, and whatever. These were photographed in Yellowstone Park in 1991. Since wolves were reintroduced there in 1995, a biologist says half the coyotes have been killed by their big cousins. Coyotes had the run of the Park before that and were not used to dealing with wolves. In Glacier Park, the natural reintroduction of wolves has cut into the hunting chances for mountain lions, so the cats have started killing the coyotes. An old Indian legend says the last sound on earth will be the howl of the coyote. Coyotes are crafty; they adapt to the worst adversities and survive. Sort of like the Chicago Cubs.*

END OF THE TRAIL *Any animal caught in a trap is not pretty. In this case, a rancher was losing newborn livestock to these creatures and was fighting back. Today in Montana and other western states, the government has a very large predator control program that uses several methods to control coyotes by shooting, trapping and poisoning. None of these activities makes happy photos, but it is part of the real world. An official report said losses were down in Montana in 1997 with only 27,000 domestic sheep killed by predators, ninety percent by coyotes. We found this trapped coyote while exploring a remote road. It had been in the trap longer than necessary, so we humanely shot it and drove on.*

BIG BULL, LITTLE HORNS *Will a bull moose just starting new spring antlers chase somebody who gets too close? We think so. A bull moose can kill a wolf with one blow from a front hoof. Doesn't need big horns to defend himself. We just sneaked a couple of fast pictures and went on our way. Does that look like a frown to you?*

UNEXPECTED *The first time we made a winter trip over Sunwapta Pass in Alberta, Canada, we were surprised to see moose up there. Most of those we know seek out low areas with plentiful willows to feed on; but these were 6,000 feet above sea level. Moose have long legs and oversized hooves, which enable them to handle deep snow better than elk or deer. The female calf in our picture is scraping through thin snow to feed on what looked like dwarf willow or similar shrub. She was with her mother and two bulls.*

Moose Milking

Rutting bull moose have tipped over everything from covered wagons to passenger cars, but have failed many times in pushing trains off the tracks. Heaven knows, it's not from lack of trying.

The moose is the largest antlered member of the deer family. It seems to have missed out on some of the congeniality genes possessed by its smaller cousins, but most moose will leave you alone if you do the same. Though bulls have caused human fatalities over the years, in most of those instances the encounter was started by the victims. One of the wildest cases happened during the fifties in Idaho. A group of loggers decided to get some moose meat with an axe and went after a bull swimming the Clearwater River. There were six men in their wooden boat; before it was over, the boat was destroyed and two of the men were killed.

Shannon recalls his own moose story, from the time one new ranger trainee was assigned to East Gate. The trainee came from the city. Soon after arriving in Yellowstone, he started getting to work late many mornings though he only had to walk a quarter of a mile. He would arrive red-faced and panting because he had been "chased by a moose." Shan believes the first time the fellow met one of the local moose, he probably was frightened and started running. With many animals, fleeing can be an irresistible come-on. All animals are able to smell and sense fear, and most have an instinct to dominate where they can. People who run sometimes attract the beasties that like to chase for fun…or for real.

Clearing trees for a roadless airstrip in the Selway Wilderness, George remembers the young man on his smokejumper crew who left the work area early each afternoon. Buzz was supposed to walk a mile to a cabin and start preparing the crew's supper. Several times a week he had to be rescued from a tree. Our crew would hear him yelling at the top of his lungs, "'Heeeeeeellllllllp!" He got so he could hold the "Help" note longer than an operatic tenor.

The trail to camp went along the edge of a lake where cow moose would stand out in the water, feeding, while leaving their calves hidden in the brush close to shore. If there was even one cow moose in the lake when it was time for Buzz to go start supper, he'd end up in a tree. We told him the moose knew he was scared of them, but he said, "No, no, they chase me because they love me." He tried to convince us he had the same problem with the "wimmin" at college.

A happy moose-related occasion was the "Moose Milking Contest" held in the wilds of Idaho during the annual Dixie Days. At least, it was supposed to be happy. An old, mostly abandoned gold mining town in the Salmon River country, Dixie is one of those places where "you can't get there from here." George attended the celebration in the summer of 1950 because he was on a Forest Service work project at the nearby Dixie Ranger Station. He flew there in an old Ford Trimotor.

There was liberal use of fermented spirits by most of the gold miners, prospectors, poachers, and river rats attending Dixie Days. In the afternoon "Moose Milking" event, contestants began staggering out of the woods and making their way to the judging area at the only bar in town. Most looked a little beat up and were carrying beer bottles that contained small amounts of white liquid. I saw no bottle with more than half a pint. One had about a teaspoon. Each team claimed to have caught and milked a cow moose to obtain the precious

READY FOR LOVE *Rocky Mountain moose are called Shiras and they are not as large as those in northern Canada and Alaska, but they get big, over a thousand pounds and up to six or seven feet at the shoulder. The world's largest antlered animals can also get rather nasty. Many is the fool-hardy man who's ended up in a tree with a moose at the bottom. Moose bulls don't have to work quite as hard as elk and deer in rounding up a mate, because the cows are usually more cooperative. In fact, they often issue "the call" and go looking for a male. On the other hand, cow moose are not thrilled by the presence of other females in the fall and can be aggressive towards their own sex.*

liquid at great personal risk and effort. Points were scored based on time and quantity. Theoretically, a team could come in later but win by having more moose juice.

That year, serious questions arose over one of the judge's qualifications. Some questioned whether he knew what moose milk tasted like. One argument led to another and there were minor fisticuff demonstrations. One grizzled gentleman was shoved over a chair and broke his bottle of white stuff. I don't know if he cried over spilled moose milk or not. The outcome was, everybody got their entry fee returned and spent it for whiskey.

To this day, I question if those guys actually caught any cow moose or whether the whole thing was staged for the benefit of the gawking city slickers who drove so many miles to take in Dixie Days. It was a good show, and at least the gold panning contest was fairly legit.

On the same topic, a few years back we bought a postcard at Jackson Hole, Wyoming, which showed a smiling man sitting on a stool and allegedly milking a cow moose. She also seemed to be smiling. Couldn't tell if he was getting any milk or not.

Fifty years ago, many saloons and gun stores out West displayed a large black-and-white photo of two skeletons lying starkly in the mountains. They were the bleached white remains of a big bull moose and a man. Among the bones were rusted remnants of a gun and knife, boots, and a leather sheath. The story going around was, the gruesome scene had been found on the east slopes of the Rockies and told the tale of a lone hunter who had mortally wounded the big bull and was then slain by the dying animal. In the 1940s, noted rifleman and writer Jack O'Conner wrote an article in *Outdoor Life* claiming the whole scenario was faked and such a thing never happened.

We still have our copy of the famous photo and wouldn't bet a nickel either way. Where men and moose are involved, anything can happen.

Left: **KILLED BY IGNORANCE** *Very few moose calves are found and brought home by people who think they're abandoned, but these were an exception. If the boys who took these from the woods had been caught by the mother, it could have been a different kind of tragedy. As it was, park rangers returned them to the wild mother but they apparently smelled so strongly of human scent she would have nothing to do with them. Too young to drink anything but mother's milk, they did die. This happened nearly forty years ago and we've not had a repeat involving moose in our area.*

Below: **BIG ENOUGH** *These calves live in dangerous country where grizzlies get a few young moose; but it's August now and they can run fast. The sun was almost down along the Shoshone River and two minutes later a big silvertip grizzly bear came ambling out of the woods and ignored the moose. While Shannon was a ranger at Yellowstone's East Gate, he was awakened by what sounded like cats meowing near his window. He peeked out...right into the eyes of a momma moose. The meowing was coming from her small twins standing near. The sound was not something expected from a large animal. It was very soft and meek.*

Left: **ONE HORN BULL** *This is a nice sized moose but he got careless last spring and badly damaged the new forming left antler. Now he just has one good one and that is a big handicap if he goes looking for love. All antlered ungulate males are very careful with the sensitive new growths coming in each spring, but stuff still happens. Maybe next year?*

Lower left: **MIGHTY BIG BABY** *While his mother is out in the brush moaning for a suitor and the males are fighting with one another, all this five-month-old calf worries about is getting regular milk from momma and finding tender water plants and rose hips for dessert. "They do grow up don't they?" Look! He's starting to get little horns already. Calf moose stay with their mother for a year. If she doesn't have another calf the following spring, she might let a daughter hang around longer.*

Below: **ANY MINUTE NOW** *Came upon a cow moose seemingly in labor near Jackson Lake, Wyoming. Were tempted to stick around but knew it was best to leave. While working for the U.S. Forest Service, George and two others watched a calf being born on a remote road. They stopped the pickup when they saw what was happening and backed up. The cow removed the birth sack from the little one, licked it all over, then charged toward the truck, so they backed up more. All newborn calves and fawns are wobbly, but it's tougher for moose because their little legs are extra long—barely get one up straight and another collapses. However, that calf was wobbling around pretty good in about twenty minutes and walked off the road. It was only then the cow stopped threatening the truck and followed her babe into the woods.*

Above: **MOOSE CITY** *Beavers are a moose's friend. This cow found lush water plants in a big dam built by those toothsome rodents. Background is part of the Livingston Range of Glacier Park, including Kinnerly Peak. Shannon climbed Kinnerly in the 1980s and left George's favorite water bottle on top. If you are ever up there, please look for one made of white plastic with a red top.*

Right: **WATCH THE EARS** *In the summer, most cow moose have a calf either with them or hidden in the brush nearby. The signal of anger is "ears back." Ears forward is a study attitude. This one is about halfway in between, so discreet withdrawal was the wise thing to do.*

Right: **THE THINKER** *What is this mulie buck doing? Some think he could be studying a colored rock or looking at a bee. The shot was made in early afternoon, so he might be just thinking about where to take a nap. He slept up on a cliff ledge last night because this is an area where lions, wolves and bears pass through. All prey species must choose bedrooms carefully. If it takes sitdown thinking, then maybe that's what he's doing.*

A three-year-old family member says, "The buck is learning to go potty." The kid could be right.

Below: **HE PREFERS WHEAT CRACKERS** *The sign says, "Keep Wildlife Wild" and it shows a deer striking a human with its front hooves. The text of the message says feeding wild animals makes them dependent on humans, sets up a possible injury to the feeder and death to the animal. In one year, half a dozen mule deer had to be removed from this one popular vista point in Glacier Park. The yearling buck standing there has undoubtedly gotten goodies here in the past or he wouldn't be hanging around.*

A MULE DEER DAY *Animals, like people, enjoy a nice winter day like this, when the sun is out after a night of fresh snow. Shannon caught these mule deer enjoying themselves at the National Bison Range.*

Above: **HIGH MOUNTAIN MOMMA** *Mule deer does in the Rockies will often have fawns near timberline. We saw this one several years in a row on Skyline Trail in Glacier. Does can be very defensive of fawns, and fight by rearing on hind legs and striking with their hard front hooves. Like their cousins the whitetails, they are also observed doing a jig on their hind legs. Don't know if they have line dancing or not.*

Above: **MULIE IDENTIFICATION** *It's easy to see the buck is a mulie because the antler tines are forked. The does have those large ears and smaller tails.*

Left: **SILLY MULIE** *Grazers and browsers are supposed to get along in the spring, but here was an exception. That mule deer buck, with his antlers still sensitive and growing, was deliberately threatening and pestering a goat that just wanted to rest in a snowbank. Deliberately antagonizing something that could kill you is dumb. However, this buck was smart enough to knock it off when he saw the billy starting to lose patience. It happened near Logan Pass on Going-to-the-Sun highway. Figured the deer might have had one too many snorts of antifreeze.*

Above: **OWEEEE!** *Even the wisest mulie buck can get surprised by chomping down on a flower with a bee inside. It does seem thoughtful of his two younger companions to act like they didn't notice his misfortune. These mule deer had survived the very bad winter and spring of 1997, so hadn't gained the sleek look they'd normally have by midsummer. However, Mother Nature balanced things out and there was an abundant supply of good grazing well into November.*

Right: **MULIE BUCK** *This guy isn't polishing his horns—already done that. He's loafin' in the sun and chewing his cud. We've never seen a mule deer buck round up a harem. They seem to run all over the mountains and prairies and try to love 'em all. Whatever works.*

Left: **WHY THE SPECKLES?** *George wrote this poem for his grandchildren:*

> Yang-gee Yang-gee yeckles, why does the fawn have freckles?
> Perhaps he has the measles or the chicken pox or spleasles.
> NO! That's not the reason. It's the baby hiding season.
> When he naps down in the bushes and doesn't move a hair.
> Nothing big can find him, not a coyote, lion or bear.
> Yang-gee yang-gee yeckles, that's why the fawn has freckles.

Below: **SPRING IS FOR FAWNS** *Whitetail does conceal their young from the world for the first few days and after that just hide them when they need to graze. A doe's first fawn is usually a single, after that fawns come in twos and sometimes threes. Like most hooved young, a fawn is almost odorless and usually can walk from the birth site in less than half an hour. George raised a male after the mother was hit by a truck. When called for supper, Pancho would come wildly racing directly at the person pouring the milk, then at the last second stop dead still, a foot from disaster. Very unnerving, and he knew it. It got worse when he got horns.*

NICE DAY *Two-and-a-half-year-old whitetail is still fat and enjoying the new snow. Whitetails yard up as the snow gets deeper, and establish trails connecting various feeding areas. They work together to break trails. Biggest unnatural hazards are crossings over high-speed roads. The worst of those are signed by highway departments, but many humans don't read well.*

LIKE A COPPER PENNY *Only a few weeks old, this fawn can run like the wind and jump a four-foot fence. Mother doesn't have to hide him anymore. Shan got this photo when he was a senior in high school. Did intense wildlife watching before pulling a hitch in the service. It had to last him three years.*

Above: **UNINHIBITED PLAYTIME** *We've not seen more joyful exuberance before or since. The mother came out on the river bank, checked the wind and everything she could see. Then on her call, two small fawns tore out of the brush and into a non-stop whirlwind of playtime. Into the bushes, out in the river, over each other's backs, whirling, kicking, leaping, twirling. It was a joy to behold and it ended too soon. When the doe signaled it was over, it stopped as suddenly as it began. The three deer melted silently into the forest.*

Right: **SAFE PLACE** *Some buck deer are smarter than others. This one knows it isn't hunting season yet, but he's picking out the best places to hang out when it does open. This is in the North Fork of the Flathead River, where most bucks head east a little ways and swim over into Glacier Park as soon as they hear a few shots go off.*

Above: **WHITETAIL BUCK** *Yup! Here's another male in training. Whitetail deer range coast-to-coast in North America, from southern Canada to Coast Rica. It is said there are now more of them than when the pilgrims landed. The secret is an obvious talent for adapting to humans, and the lack of predators. They are hunted heavily in Montana, yet thousands are hit each year by cars. We see them on the streets. They're probably in the yard right now eating our apples. On the other hand, they keep spreading into high country and we've seen them at timber line in Glacier National Park during the last few years.*

Left: **LAST FIGHT** *This is the way a relatively few whitetail buck battles end. Usually when it happens one buck dies first. We know of instances where someone found such unlucky deer and freed the live one, but it wasn't easy. An angry or frightened buck can be very dangerous to get near. In this case, the left horn of the buck on the left penetrated the skull of the other and they were locked. Dozens of creatures such as ravens, moles, coyotes, weasels and even chickadees seem to get word of things like this and the carcasses are consumed in a few days. After that come mice, beetles and ants. Nature works.*

BLACK BEARS

Packer Beats the Bear

George has never forgotten Packer Cliff's run-in with a black bear. Those creatures may be called the clowns of the woods, but they can also be dangerous when they want.

During the Big War, a teenaged George worked in the wilderness at Elk Park Ranger Station. A middle-sized black bear began raiding the garbage pit, an eight-foot hole in the ground with slabs across the top. The crew there were high school boys except for two others: an older fella who cooked, and "Packer" Cliff.

Packers ran the mule and horse strings that supplied food and equipment to fire lookouts and trail crews. Our Cliff was probably in his forties, not too tall but tougher than an old boot. He talked out the side of his mouth, cussed a blue streak, and made it clear to us "punk kids" he wasn't afraid to fight a grizzly with a switch.

We were eating supper one night when the cook looked out the window and said the bear had just gone down in the garbage pit again. Packer slammed his fist so hard against the table that all our plates jumped. He leaped from his chair saying, "I'll fix that %&*#@ S.O.B. so he'll never come back." Pulling his battered cowboy hat down to his ears, out the door he went, calling that bear names we boys had never heard before.

Just as he reached the garbage pit the bear came barreling out, headed for the timber a couple hundred yards away, with Packer right on his heels. From the rear, a black bear in a hurry is hilarious because of the way its hind legs come clear past its ears, and Packer's churning bowlegs looked like a high-speed eggbeater. Bowlegged or not, Packer Cliff could run.

The terrified bear must have thought the banshees from hell were on its tail and gaining. As it went past the one big tree in the meadow, it desperately threw out its left front paw to grab the trunk. With the bear's great momentum the bark pulled loose so, instead of going up, the bear felt a sudden jerk that spun him around the tree. At that exact second Packer came zooming in from the other side. Bear and man collided in a whirling blur of fur, arms, legs, and Levis. A ten-gallon hat flew in the air.

Watching from the porch, we all stopped laughing for a second, until we could see the terrified bear breaking all records for tree climbing. Out of the dust at the bottom of the trunk came Packer Cliff. He was heading back, maybe even faster than he had left.

Cookie was chuckling, too, but he said, "We better get back inside and eat the supper I fixed." It was silent as we ate, except for Packer's puffing. After he got his wind back, he broke the silence. "I'll tell you punk kids somethin'," he said. "That's the first %#&*@ bear ever had the guts to take me on."

Left: **THE LITTLEST VICTIM** *This baby bear learned the wrong things from the day it came out of the den. It seems very difficult for many people to refrain from feeding such a cute little guy pleading for chips or a sack of Oreos. But bears do just fine without human handouts.*

Below: **VICTIMS OF KINDNESS** *We worried about these two the first time we saw them on Camas Road in Glacier Park, because the mother was bumming food from tourists. Both had to be trapped and moved when she began getting aggressive if visitors didn't hand over goodies. In the transplant operation, the cub died; the female had to be shot later that summer when she returned to Camas Road and her aggressive ways. Feeding bears anywhere is usually a death sentence to them...now or later.*

Right: **BEGGAR BEARS OF YORE** *George saw people feeding bears in Glacier on his first visit in 1936, and they were still at it when he snapped this in 1961. But not long after, with tourist injuries mounting and "bear jams" tying up traffic, the government started enforcing no-feeding rules, and increased fines. Many bears had to be killed when they couldn't make the necessary dietary adjustment. Still, a problem is training people to understand, "When you give a bear your last hot dog, it might like fifty more." In the spring of 1998, Yosemite National Park rangers were warning of California bears that had learned how to rip off car doors if they smelled food inside.*

Right: **WATCH FOR A DARK SPOT** *Were on a hiking trip in Glacier with a lady who'd never seen a wild bear. Told her to watch for something darker than its surroundings, "Like that blob down there in the clearing. Sometimes if you watch long enough you'll swear you saw it move." She replied, "Okay, I'll look through the binoculars...Oh! It really did move." We took another look and sure enough, that one spot had turned into a mother black bear with two cubs. She must have been nursing them when there was only one blob.*

Above: **HOW TO BE A COOL GOAT** *Even though these mountain goats have shed their long winter coats, there is still too much heat for them in mid-summer. That is why they wiggle and snuggle into a snow bank every chance they get. If you want to see these cliff-walkers in the summer, look in shaded areas during the heat of the day. They seem pleased if the temperature drops to freezing and it starts to snow in July or August. That's because they are built to handle fifty below zero. You seldom see them naturally below elevations of 6,000 feet.*

Right: **IT'S RESTING TIME** *The most popular mountain goat watching area in the world is near Logan Pass in Glacier Park. This bored billy could have picked a better spot to relax and chew his cud. There are a million acres nearby with no tourists around. A few goats hang out here to lap up antifreeze, which leaks from overheated vehicles. Veterinarians say it's cumulative in their systems and can cause serious illness, but the park has not found evidence of any dying from this addictive habit.*

MOUNTAIN GOATS

The Taster Tester

Dinner time and the following hours of alpine glow among the peaks is conversation time at the rustic Sperry Chalet in Glacier National Park. Besides being a hikers' heaven, perched on a clifftop just under the Continental Divide, Sperry Chalet is right in the middle of a large, healthy mountain goat population. Many good stories circulate up there as the climbers and hikers gather at the dining hall tables and share their day's adventures.

One of the best came from the late Hal Kanzler, a great climbing companion and one of those most responsible for my interest in wildlife photography. A big challenge of wildlife picture-taking is getting the subject with a nice background. We all dream of the ideal shot where the animal is perfectly lit, in a great pose, and with beautiful peaks in the background, or maybe an alpine lake far below.

Many years ago, Hal hiked to Lincoln Pass, just southeast of Sperry Chalet, because that area has it all: towering peaks, glaciers, and lakes. There were goats nearby, but none was in the right spot, not out there on the ledges where the spectacular background could be included. Hal had his two boys, Jimmy and Jerry, along, and he told them, "We are all going to go wee wee on this rock." The boys wanted to know why, so Hal explained, "Human urine contains sodium, chloride, potassium, urea and nitrogen. In fact, scientists make urea from synthesized ammonia and carbon dioxide, to use in manufacturing animal feed. This rock is in a good location. It also has lichen and moss on it, so will soak up and hold the moisture longer. I'm sure we can lure in some goats."

It worked like a charm. After Hal and the boys got their photos, they went on to other adventures along the trail to Gunsight Pass and Lake Ellen Wilson.

The evening dinner crowd happened to include one of those irritating fellows who knows more than anyone else on any given subject. He had a strident voice used to dominate the conversation at his own table, and the rest of those in the room as well.

Mr. Knowitall wanted everyone to hear about his alleged close call with a giant grizzly bear and a near fall into a crevasse on the glacier, but he saved his goat story until last and insisted upon having everyone's attention.

"Today I've made a discovery which could have far-reaching impacts on biological studies of the mountain goat. As I approached the top of Lincoln Pass, where you look eastward to the lakes and waterfalls, I was absolutely amazed to see several goats jostling each other over one particular rock. They were voraciously licking the surface, which included lichen and some moss. Even though there were other rocks just like the one they were licking, they completely ignored them."

Hal forcefully broke in, "Excuse me, Mr. Knowitall. Were you able to determine what the attraction was?"

"No, sir! I did not, but I did several things which should help solve the mystery. Driving the goats away for a few minutes, I carefully examed the rock's entire surface and for a time employed my field magnification glass. Using a pocket kanife, I then carefully cut and pried loose a patch of moss and lichen that seemed to be getting the goats' closest attention. A part of that sample is now sealed in my pack and will be subjected to close laboratory examination when I return to the east."

Hal had another question: "What did you do with the remaining sample you removed from the rock?"

"Well, I did the only thing an intelligent, educated person would do under the circumstances. On the way back from the pass, I tasted and carefully chewed some of the moss and the lichen. Having not eaten any of that sort of thing before, I could not be sure what detectable flavors might be different from regular moss and lichen…so I am going back up there in the morning, and do comparison taste tests between the goat rock and others nearby."

It was Jerry's turn to get in to the conversation, but he just whispered in Hal's ear. "Gee, Dad! Aren't you going to tell him we all peed on that rock?"

"No," Hal whispered back. "If he actually gets a laboratory analysis of the sample, he may eventually find out what happened up there in Lincoln Pass. In the meantime, I want you and your brother to knock off that giggling."

Above: **THE LAST SUMMER?** *In 1992, George and his hiking group, The Over-the-Hill-Gang, climbed Bear Hat Mountain on the Continental Divide near Logan Pass and saw a huge old goat that just had nubbins left of his horns. He climbed down a ways with us and even joined us in a short rest. We all figured he'd never make it through the next winter. But in early summer of 1993, we were in the same area and ran into this old fellow with the telltale nubbin horns. We've since wondered if this was the same giant billy Shannon and I saw in 1990. No way of knowing for sure, but it could be.*

Left: **NEW WINTER COATS** *The first autumn snows have fallen in the high country, but this nanny and her kid are fattened up from a summer of feeding, and their long winter hair with underfur keeps them warm. The billies spar around in the fall mating season, but knowing the other guy has very sharp horns, they don't get too serious about it, mainly just jab each other in the behind. That doesn't seem too unreasonable.*

DON'T LOOK DOWN *Would you take your little kid out there? Twelve goats were on this cliff when Shan took the picture, several above that nanny and kid, top center. The mother with two little ones at lower right is just heading up. We chose this particular shot to show the roaring river directly below. The goats have gathered here on Glacier Park's southern edge for centuries to satisfy a need for salt in their diet. The largest gathering is in spring. Many tourists visit, along with a few local mountain lions.*

Left: **GOATS IN DECEMBER** *A nanny and her kid are doing fine on Glacier's Garden Wall. They have caves and cliffs for staying out of bad winds, and then go out on cleared ridges to feed. The terrible winter of '95-'96 seemed to affect the goats the least. Regular winters are no sweat. There were places up here where over forty feet of snow fell during the bad winter, but prevailing winds roaring over the Continental Divide blew much of it clear to North Dakota.*

Right: **A YOGA GOAT** *Deep meditation, stretching and controlled breathing. Watched this goat high on a mountain knowing he didn't know yoga, but he was doing something sorta ritualistic. No animal to our knowledge maintains greater physical fitness than a mountain goat. George learned that the hard way. Sat up late with friends in the kitchen of the remote Sperry Chalet and had to make my way to the sleeping building on a narrow walk. Found passage blocked by the rear end of an adult goat. Without thinking, I raised my hand in the air and whacked him hard on the rump. Two things happened instantly. He switched ends so I was looking at two black daggers, and every bone in my hand felt broken. Rocks are softer.*

Left: **THE BIGGEST GOAT** *Shannon and George both believe this is the biggest mountain goat they ever saw. We had climbed Mt. Clements in August of 1990 and were returning to Logan Pass when this huge fellow came down from cliffs to cool off in the snow. He was massive enough to startle us at first sight. He was obviously up in years, but showed no decline in physical condition—looked like he could handle any billy that ever lived.*

Above: **BRAND NEW KID** *Momma's old coat looks awful but the new baby doesn't care. He is busy learning to climb and play king-of-the-hill. Mountain goats have special anti-skid pads on their feet and the knee is low down so they can use front legs as a hook to get up ledges.*

Left: **GOAT HEAVEN** *Why would a goat like this place? Simple! It offers plentiful natural food, protection from the afternoon sun, wide view of surroundings, cliffs nearby to escape predators, and creek only a thousand feet below. There is at least one nanny with her little kid, and two others in the photo's center. Super eyes might find a couple more. Most goats figure places like this are better than hanging around tourists at Logan Pass and getting hooked on antifreeze.*

Above left: **LEARNING FAST**
This kid has lived through June and July without falling off that 800-foot cliff right behind him. Some don't live that long. The mother goats always lie down between their kids and the cliff's edge during naps and rest periods, but still a high percentage of babies don't make it until the following spring. That is a natural peril for animals living in a world so straight up and down.

Above right: **WHERE HAVE YOU BEEN, BILLY BOY?** *Goats in the high places are usually quite shy, but this young one came right over to visit during one of our July climbs on Mt. Gould in Glacier Park. Billies shed their long winter coats earlier than the females, and this one has already started his new one. It sounds sort of silly, but this guy actually seemed glad to see us. Look at that sparkle in his eye.*

Above: **BARELY BELIEVABLE** *People have asked about the goat head on a tree. That unfortunate fellow accidentally sat in a puddle of sticky pine pitch. The awful stuff worked down to the skin and began to itch, so the goat backed up to the nearest tree and started scratching his rump. Back and forth, scratch, scratch, scratch. We watched him scratch until dark. Came back three days later and that is all that was left.*

PRONGHORNS

THE LATEST SPEEDSTER *This pronghorn fawn was standing up ten minutes after being born, trying to nurse. As soon as the doe got it cleaned, she had another one. She left them lying on the ground for about half an hour before all three left. Wild mothers instinctively know to not stay near the birthing area because it could attract predators. We saw the trio later that day two miles away, and the fawns were bobbing along like two cotton balls. These fawns act similar to human kids in that they go three times as far as needed to get some place. Have no desire to go even twenty feet in a straight line. Must be a thing to get them maximum exercise.*

TEN MINUTES OLD *The firstborn twin waits in the wild maternity ward while its sibling comes into the world on Wild Horse Mesa, National Bison Range. Babe May has a photo of one antelope fawn nursing while the other twin was being born. This one waited a few minutes. These little guys are much more colorful once they get dried off.*

Right: **DANGER SIGNAL** *All pronghorns (commonly called antelope), even the fawns, send danger warnings by instantly raising the long white hair on their rumps. The action resembles the opening of a flower when observed from this vantage point. The sharp-eyed pronghorns can read this signal for miles. We surprised this buck and doe at close range and they both flashed the danger sign. Got two pictures and within seconds they were far away. They can just flat-out fly. He is a young buck and is dang lucky to get one girlfriend. The big bucks round up harems of ten or more.*

Below: **FASTEST ANIMAL ALIVE?** *There is argument based on nebulous data as to a pronghorn being able to outrun a cheetah. We don't know. Scientists say the pronghorn developed its famous gait many years ago to survive in a prehistoric time when now extinct predators were still around. Once barely hanging on with unhuntable populations, the shy pronghorn is now common throughout the west. Watching them run is a joy. In areas where they were not hunted, we've had them race our car, apparently just for fun. George's dad clocked one at 62 miles per hour.*

Above: **BLUE GROUSE DANDY** *For a normally drab bird, a male blue grouse chasing females can sure get gussied up. Eyebrows turn bright red-orange. Red neck gland swells up and are framed with contrasting white feathers, and the fanned-out tail is really something. In early spring near snow line, these guys establish courtin' territory and put on a heck of a song and dance show to lure in the ladies. What may be singing to them is sort of a Rocky Mountain rap.*

Above: **THE FLOWERS THAT FLY** *Bluebirds throughout the hemisphere have made a cheering return to significant numbers, thanks to the tireless work of "Bluebird Trail" volunteers. We now see these azure thrushes above timberline near glaciers, across the high prairies and into lowland valleys. The mountain bluebirds like this male are the bluest of all and they seem to sing only of sunshine and happiness.*

Right: **THE SMALLEST HAWK** *Kestrels are hunters that feed on large insects such as grass-hoppers, but probably prefer small birds, mice and little snakes when they can catch them. We find them the most colorful of all American birds of prey, but they're shy and hard to photograph.*

BIRDS

The Flowers That Fly

There were too few living colors in George's early life. Dry-land homesteads were drab, and the thin soil at Camas Prairie did not support lawns, domestic flowers, or gardens. He knew nothing of white picket fences with red roses. Perhaps that is what developed his life-long awe of magic things that come with spring.

There were scattered blooms of bitterroot and camas in our childhood, but the most heartening colors of our world arrived with the mountain bluebirds. Abetting and contrasting their azure brightness were meadowlarks with glowing yellow vests marked by black vees. Bluebirds and larks lit up our hardscrabble lives. Free, exquisite jewels accenting the joy of living, they sang their hearts out each day to earth and sky.

As the years slipped away, so did the bluebirds. I occasionally saw some, but not enough to bring back those little-boy days of the thirties, and memories faded while those beautiful thrushes grew fewer and fewer.

On a crisp fall morning in the late sixties, I wandered alone to a remote forest meadow as the sun rose over the snowy peaks of Glacier Park. The scene was one I had never witnessed before, and never have since. It took a moment to comprehend how that autumn-browned expanse had blossomed overnight with a brilliant blue. It soon sunk in: the flowers were birds. Hundreds upon hundreds of mountain bluebirds were perching, hovering, and flitting before my eyes. The dawn sun reflected deep, glowing cobalt wings and azure pelage with lighter tints of cerulean and indigo. Here were acres of dazzling "flowers that could fly," and I wondered, "Where did they come from? How did they meet here?"

Running to the cabin for a camera proved fruitless, because I returned to emptiness. The rarest of magic shows had vanished, and I was left with, "Where have they gone?" One thought thrilled me. "There are still bluebirds," I told myself. I fought down my frustration at not getting photos with memories of a migration I never knew existed.

Since then, I've learned that replacing pioneer wooden fences with treated or metal posts removed the nesting cavities needed by the birds, and clearing more and more tree lands took away dead snags where woodpeckers had for centuries made homes that bluebirds later filled. Over the last quarter of a century, thoughtful people have begun building "birdhouse trails" across the United States and Canada. It is only in recent years that I have learned about the breadth and success of their work.

On March 25, 1998, driving along Highway 28 in western Montana, through the Big Draw, it hit me: the flying flowers were everywhere. Shannon and I took a few moments to watch them near birdhouses on posts. Then, on a hunch, I took Route 382 over the hill to Camas Prairie. It, too, is lined with bluebird "apartments," and many were occupied. Seeing those birds made our day.

We began seeking out the wonderful local people who had brought the bluebirds back. Led by Art Aylesworth of Ronan, Montana, and retired school principal Irwin Davis, a local "Mountain Bluebird Trails" club has since 1973 erected more than 28,000 of those specially designed boxes. On the day I talked to Irwin he had banded 130 of the birds; his club is working with scholars at Cornell University, along with other scientists, to learn more about the beautiful little singers. Even today, the biggest mystery is exactly how and where they go in winter. "There are some guesses," Irwin says, "but nobody really knows."

Henry David Thoreau said, "The bluebird carries the sky on his back." One of my favorite childhood songs described a hobo paradise equipped with "lemonade springs where the bluebird sings." Robert Frost wrote of

the north wind making a beloved bluebird vanish, but held out hope: "Perhaps in the Spring, He would come back and sing."

One of my little brothers is the first person I recall telling me, some sixty years ago, "Da pretty blue flower flied away." I've since learned that of the three bluebird species, only the mountain bluebird, which summers here, is able to hover. It is while performing this unique action that it most resembles a dazzling flower, rustled by the wind. The male and female birds also use fluttering wing gestures to signal to each other.

There are many things humans do not know about these soft, warbling, bluer-than-blue thrushes, especially where they go in the cold seasons. Perhaps Dorothy in the *Wizard of Oz* had it right when she sang, "Somewhere, over the rainbow, bluebirds fly."

NEST ON THE ROCKS *Big rocks, little rocks, low ones and tall, that is where Canada geese nest on the Upper Madison River. Why? Because the banks are patrolled by coyotes, mink and other pesky varmints and good nesting trees are scarce. We have shots of the mother on the eggs, but this one shows action. She made a short honking circle of the area and came right back. Some of the geese in Yellowstone migrate south, a few stay all winter.*

Right: **TIME TO CHANGE** *Almost stepped on a ptarmigan in early spring tundra and it did the unthinkable—walked off the snow. It didn't stay long on this contrasting background because it knows better. The all-white little grouse will begin the color change of feathers within days, before the snow melts.*

Left: **IS SHE IMPRESSED?** *We've watched the blue grouse rituals over the years and have never detected actual passion or excitement from the blue ladies. This one was watching the show and would blink once in a while. Must work. There were baby grouse a little later.*

Right: **GOOD CAMOUFLAGE** *Ptarmigan chicks are mottled to match the summer alpine country where they live. In winter these tundra grouse turn white, and in spring and fall are about fifty-fifty. Their protective coloring saves them from high country eagles and other predators. We've seen a mother get her whole brood of four or five chicks safely through a summer. They live above treeline, feeding on dwarf willow and other plants.*

NOT GOOD FATHERS *Like most ducks, the beautiful male wood ducks leave raising the young to the mother hens. Sure, they stick around after the nesting starts, but they're no real help. After the eggs hatch—usually up in a hollow tree—the little ones literally fall to the ground and waddle to the nearest pond or lake with the mother. They seem able to fall a long ways without getting hurt, probably because they're so light and fluffy. In this picture, the drake on the right may be from the summer hatch, and he has caught up with the ol' man to see what's new in the men's world.*

ROBBER RAVEN *A little girl was drinking this soda but the raven flew down and took it away. It was too heavy to carry up in a tree, so he sat on a stump and dared anyone to retrieve it. This bird was raised at a hunting lodge in British Columbia and moved down to our cabin near the border. The next day, while George was working on a motorcycle, it kept butting in. We thought he wanted to help until he tried to steal a shiny wrench.*

Shannon says these are the smartest birds around. One named TukTuk lived near his mouse-infested cabin in Yellowstone and Shan began feeding it mice caught in traps. Didn't leave any on the porch one night and was awakened at five a.m. by loud pounding on the tin roof. Got up and there was the raven, very upset. Shan went back to bed, but no use. Had to give the bird two eggs in order to get some sleep. TukTuk pounded every morning for three days before accepting defeat. The raven also liked sitting on a rock cawing until a ranger's dog would chase it so TukTuk could zoom back and steal dog food. One time there was a bull buffalo feeding nearby, so once he got the dog chasing him, TukTuk flew low to the ground right toward the bull, barely missing its back. This caused the dog to almost crash full tilt into the bull. Shannon believes it was all a planned deal.

THE DARING CLOWNS *Few ducks are as beautifully colored as the male harlequin and few as mysterious. They arrive in very early spring at the wildest mountain streams. They calmly dive into roaring maelstroms for food. Don't know how they come out alive. Males arrive first and set up courting stretches of water. They seem to be great friends until the females arrive. Once the mating is over and the hens are nesting, these lotharios take off. The hen raises the little fuzzies by herself and when they get big enough to feed alone, she takes off. How these young ones find their way hundreds and sometimes thousands of miles to the ocean wintering areas of their parents is a super mind-boggler. Talk about "tough love"!*

Left: **THE WOODLAND DRUMMER** *Male ruffed grouse beat their own drums. You can hear them in the spring, calling to all unattached ladies from shady glens. For years, people thought the sound came from the rapid wing beats hitting a log, but now we figure it's the wings and body. Calling in a gal is only half the work, apparently, because they'll keep drumming after a potential mate shows up. She sits there watching his style. No self-respecting lady wants to hook up with a lousy drummer. Because grouse live in places used by hunting hawks, owls and predators like wildcats, grouse have a lower life expectancy than waterfowl. Five years would probably be ancient.*

Left: **THE HAWK THAT FISHES** *Osprey dive from high in the air to grab fish swimming near the surface. They prefer catching prey from the rear so the fish is aerodynamic during the flight to the nest. We found this young adult sitting sick on the bank of a "wild river," and brought him home for treatment. He couldn't fly or work his talons, but antibiotics seems to bring him around. "Ozzie" was almost ready for release when he died of an unknown cause.*

Below: **WORLD TRAVELER** *Osprey around the world migrate up to thousands of miles. They nest near water where the fishing is good and they have increased in numbers the last twenty years. Once in a while an osprey will drop a fish while flying, and a local man was almost hit on the head by a falling rainbow trout. We caught a fifteen-inch cutthroat trout in Glacier Park that had been dropped back into the lake. The deep talon wounds had almost healed. Not many fish that lucky.*

Above: **HONKERS IN HIGH COUNTRY** *We were making an early spring climb near the Continental Divide in Glacier Park. Suddenly heard geese honking all around— sounded like a political convention. We located half a dozen V formations circling and talking to each other, apparently looking for a pass through the cloud-topped peaks to the east. There are two squadrons smack dab in the middle of this photo, flying right to left. Their decision was to go back west toward the valley until the divide cleared off. View is west and snowy thing at right is Heavens Peak.*

Above right: **MAGPIE** *There are 144 species of land birds that nest in the Northern Rockies then migrate to the neotropics. This isn't one. A despised bird among western ranchers, the magpie is another survivor, a wild thing designated by nature as a scavenger and a predator. Their biggest sin is attacking helpless living things. Other than that they can be entertaining and pretty.*

Center: **CANADA JAY** *Camp robbers, they are called. This naturally shy Canada jay steals food from hikers and campers clear to the arctic circle. When they can't get human treats, they get by just fine on natural foods. See 'em pecking evergreen cones a lot. They live in high forest country and like to talk. Probably lonely.*

Right: **GIRL NAMED HAGAR** *People reported this great horned owl lying in a highway ditch after it hit a power line. We rescued it and named it Hagar before knowing he was a her. She lived several years but was never able to fly well enough to hunt. Wild males came to her big cage and hooted sweet nothings. You can see she was a "looker." Great horned owls are strong, silent hunters with built-in radar and night vision. Hagar ran talons completely through George's hand while we were splinting its wing. Shannon pried them out one at a time and blocked re-entry with pencils. Hagar was killed and eaten by a wild mink, we think.*

Left: **LITTLEST OWL** *There are several species of small owls. Think this one is a northern saw-whet. It appears to be a juvenile with a head injury—one pupil is much larger than the other. It was turned over to a skilled woman who has government permission to care for injured creatures. A big saw-whet might weigh four ounces and stand eight inches. Main diet is mice and their call is a plain old "toot toot toot."*

Below: **SWALLOW'S SWALLOWERS** *How'd you like to be a parent and get this greeting when you came home from work? Swallows are swift flyers, catching hundreds of flying insects per day. The parents make dozens of trips each hour with a beak full of bugs.*

Above: **BALD EAGLES** *Our national symbol has dignity and fierceness in his face, but we've seen him embarrassed. Watched one at Lake McDonald trying to catch a wild duck by circling overhead then swooping down. Each time he drew close the duck would dive under the water and the eagle would have to hit full air brakes and fly back up for another try. The duck was wise enough to know if she flew, she was a goner. On about the sixth attempt, the duck waited until the last possible moment to submerge and the diving eagle crashed in the water after it. Spray flew high in the air. We thought he had the duck, but that intended supper came up thirty feet away. It took perhaps fifteen minutes for the eagle to get dried out enough to fly again, and the duck with pre-oiled feathers was long gone.*

Top right: **THE EAGLE TREE** *For decades there were spawning runs of silver salmon in McDonald Creek on the west side of Glacier Park. Up to 500 eagles would fly in from hundreds of miles away each fall to get in on the goodies. We used to sneak through the woods and watch them catch fish, fight over fish, and sit in trees. This big old cottonwood was the favorite. Our highest count at one time was thirty-four in the Eagle Tree. An experimental plant of freshwater shrimp upset things, and the salmon soon were gone. The eagles went elsewhere and the tree fell, but we have this 1965 photo.*

Right: **EAGLE IN WINTER** *The American bald eagle does not join others in migrating to a better climate. A pair of them will stay married for years and nest in the same place; however, we do know of at least one female who had a fling with a traveling stranger. It caused a big scandal around the Lake McDonald Lodge back in the eighties. As to this eagle, it is watching for anything huntable near the outlet of St. Mary's Lake, eastern boundary of Glacier Park.*

Above: **FURRY TORPEDOES** *River otters seem to be the happiest animals we've observed. While fly fishing, we heard a mother and two young ones coming because they were laughing as they came 'round the bend, frolicking all the way. Otters move through the water extremely fast when they want to catch their principal food, which is fish. Sliding down banks of mud, grass or snow is a favorite pastime and they'll do it over and over again. They'd go nuts at Disneyland. They are more family-oriented than most furbearers; however, the female does kick the male out of the streamside burrow for a few days right after the babies are born. He comes back in a short time and helps raise them.*

While fishing a small lake, an otter followed Shannon for an hour, never getting closer than ten yards but obviously enjoying some company. Conversely, Shan met a wolverine on the trail while hunting in deep snow and the wolverine expressed great anger at having to give way. If it was genetically possible to have a hybrid otter-wolverine, it would be terribly neurotic.

Left: **WINTER WATER OTTERS** *Playful? You bet. These two swam toward us then burrowed under the four feet of snow we were standing in and popped up a few feet from Shannon and his friend Mike Schlegel. We were flabbergasted. Didn't get one picture. It was at least two hundred feet from the river bank and they covered that distance in a minute. Most surprising thing to us was how they knew where to come up. Maybe they heard talking. Probably George.*

MORE CRITTERS

ON THE PROWL *Male mountain lions will join up with any female at any time of the year, but late winter is the usual female choice. Males don't help raise the kittens. These panthers do not like to feed on carrion and prefer eating only what they have downed themselves. This one was caught as a kitten and raised by a former sheriff who claimed to use him guarding prisoners. Of course, that was before the ACLU got so persnickety.*

MEANEST CRITTER IN THE WOODS *If things are going well for a wolverine, it probably gets mad. The babies are ornery and get worse each day. Ancient Indians called them "devil bear." We know about their destructive raids on cabins, trap lines and food caches. Ravaged things that are not edible, they'll tear up or foul with bad-smelling musk. There are stories of them even driving grizzly bears from a carcass. For a member of the weasel family, they get big—up to fifty pounds. Wolverines can kill animals much bigger than they are.*

Humans seldom see these magnificent fighting machines in the wild, and the one time we were close enough to get a good picture, George had his film loaded wrong. Have only heard their talk a few times and if we had to describe the sound with one word, it would be "malevolent." Climbing through Bird Woman Cirque in Glacier Park, we ran into one and he threatened us with facial and vocal menacing, but always stayed a hundred yards or so away. After we reached the open ridge top and were resting, it patrolled back and forth in the timber below still making that unforgettably haunting, mean, lonely sound. In their book Montana Wildlife, *Bert Gildart and Jan Wassink called the wolverine the "greatest troublemaker in the animal world." They're probably right.*

Our wolverine photo was taken by Shannon at an Edmonton, Alberta, game farm.

ALPINE FARMER *Pikas are the darndest little animals of the high country. They are cuter than a bug's ear, live in colonies near and above timberline, and spend most of their lives in dark burrows under vast piles of rocks. Short summers are pikas' time to shine and they take advantage of every single moment. They play a little bit but work very hard gathering grass, leaves and flowers which they cure into hay on rocks. When rain clouds threaten, all the drying hay is rushed under cover, then brought back out when the sun returns. Cured hay is stored underground and eaten all winter because pikas do not go into hibernation sleep like many other animals in frigid zones.*

We've wondered why biologists and psychiatrists haven't studied these animals more, because they possess very unique body water disposal systems that might be utilized in medical research for humans. Their urine is said to be crystal clear. Psychologists could find out how so many residents get along, cramped up in the dark for eight or nine months straight. We've noticed how just a few weeks snowbound in a log cabin can make a couple of the most jovial humans turn "shack nasty."

CHAMPION DIGGER *Badgers spend their lives digging into burrows where gophers, ground squirrels and prairie dogs live, because that's what they eat. In good digging ground, we've seen these long-clawed things go out of sight from a flat start in a minute. Talk about a hairy roto-rooter. The dirt really flies. They prefer to fight with just their front claws and sharp teeth showing in a hole.*

Caught in the open with no time to dig, the badger raises its hair to look bigger and snarls at the intruder. Few animals will risk a fight with a badger. They're all business...no sense of humor. The fluffy one here charged George, who snapped a picture and ran. Think she had babies nearby.

SNOWSHOE RABBIT *Technically, this is a hare, right on the bottom of the food chain, but they've enough going for them to keep on hopping through the ages. In courting they will stand on their hind legs and box with opponents. We've watched the courting and it is a madhouse of wild chases, jumping, boxing...and stuff. Snowshoe hares are white in winter. Besides having good camouflage, they run very fast, jump twenty feet, have great hearing, eyesight, and smell. Populations of lynx and other predators go up and down in relation to the numbers of these prey animals, another of nature's mysterious checks and balances.*

Above left: **HARD-WORKING HOARDER** *Nobody stores away as much food for winter as the western red, or pine, squirrel. They also chatter a great deal. They consider it their duty to warn any other bird or animal if a large creature is moving through the area. Not being a hibernator, these small creatures bury coniferous nuts all around their homes in trees, and come down most winter days to dig up something tasty. They get hunted a lot, and their worst enemy is the pine marten. Squirrels raise a couple of small families each year. They play a lot.*

Above right: **WESTERN RATTLER** *Here is about four feet of bad news if you're a gopher. He's not good news to a human who steps on him. The western rattlesnake seldom gets over five feet long, but can be trouble at any length. We don't see many, but that's all right with us. The rattlesnake was so much trouble to early-day settlers that their numbers were greatly reduced, especially around homesteads and settlements. Grandpa Ostrom told us that when they were pulling into their homestead claim on the prairie, a big rattler struck at the lead horse of the covered wagon. The horse jumped aside, causing the snake fangs to hit the wagon tongue and it swelled up so big they sawed off enough lumber to build their first cabin.*

Center: **ALBINO CRITTERS** *A genetic quirk creates albino animals, including Columbia ground squirrels like this one. They lack the pigment for normal coloring of hair and skin. Such creatures start life with a strike against them, especially if they are a prey species, because they are much more visible to predators. We know of pure white, pink-eyed animals being sighted among just about every kind of living creature including deer, bears, bluebirds, and human beings. A hawk flying over a colony of ground squirrels isn't going to have much trouble spotting this one. On the positive side, enough somehow survive to keep the genes going. Maybe some albinos realize they are different and stick closer to the burrow.*

Left: **LITTLE BIG CHIPMUNK** *The golden mantle chipmunk— ground squirrel to some—is usually seen in the high country, but this baby belongs to a family that has been illegally fed by humans. Why else would it be sitting at a national park bus stop looking so cute?*

UNTAMABLE KITTENS *Some people say you can tame a wildcat, but we're not going to try it. When these bobcats get full grown they will have razor sharp retractable claws and more sharp teeth than you care to meet. They are shy, very curious, seldom seen by humans. We are proud of our work in helping to get them some legal protection here in Montana. Surprised one at night sneaking some meat from the roof of our cabin. The hissing, snarling and spitting was enough to scare us back inside, and we're not afraid of anything.*

BAD NAME *The ultimate insult in early Western movies was calling somebody a "yellow belly," but that's this creature's name. Marmots are bushy-tailed woodchucks and there are several kinds. High in the Rockies dwells the hoary marmot that turns silver color as it ages. The yellow-bellied marmot will have a yellow belly all his life. They spend almost three fourths of their time hibernating in the high country, and grizzly bears dig them out of burrows—or at least try. Sometimes hours of digging prove in vain and the marmot wins.*

A TREE DWELLER *Pine martens are shy, have cute faces and can run through trees at top speed. They are very inquisitive so were easy to trap to near extinction in the olden days for their beautiful pelts. They prey chiefly on squirrels. We've had them follow us in the wilderness on rare occasions, mostly young ones. This bright-eyed adult was watching a Steller's jay pecking dried berries. Would a marten eat a blue jay? Could happen.*

ABOUT THE AUTHORS

Shannon Ostrom served five years as a seasonal ranger in Yellowstone National Park, and currently works at Glacier National Park, where he grew up hiking, mountain climbing, and watching wildlife. He served three years in the U.S. Army climbing in the Alps and traveling in Europe and Africa. Did a stint with the NATO Forces above the Arctic Circle in Norway and was on an army ski team. Returning home, he operated summer sightseeing boats in Glacier while studying at Montana State University. Shannon has been progressively handicapped by myotonic muscular distrophy but still made trips the last few years, including photo-adventures to Alaska, Canada, Hawaii, and in 1998 a Costa Rican jungle with brother Clark and father George.

G. George Ostrom calls himself "the oldest living reporter." He's been in that business over sixty years at some level, currently as News Director at Radio KOFI in Kalispell, Montana. He has owned and operated a weekly newspaper and a radio station, contributed articles and photos to national magazines from *Sports Illustrated* to the *Saturday Evening Post*, and written a newspaper column for thirty-five years in the Pulitzer Prize–winning *Hungry Horse News*. George has won state, regional, and national writing awards. His inspiration for the camera hobby grew from early association with noted photographers Hal Kanzler and Danny On. He and On met as fire smoke-jumpers after World War II.

His first book, *Glacier's Secrets*, tells of the weekly Glacier Park climbs of The Over the Hill Gang, to which George still belongs.